D0198084

AQ2016
AAT ADVANCED DIPLOMA IN ACCOUNTING LEVEL 3

QUESTION BANK

Final Accounts Preparation

2016 Edition

For assessments from September 2016

First edition June 2016

ISBN 9781 4727 4850 8

British Library Cataloguing-in-Publication Data
A catalogue record for this book is available from the British Library

Published by

BPP Learning Media Ltd
BPP House, Aldine Place
142-144 Uxbridge Road
London W12 8AA

www.bpp.com/learningmedia

Printed in the United Kingdom by Ashford Colour Press Ltd.

Unit 600, Fareham Reach,
Fareham Road
Gosport, Hampshire
PO13 0FW

Your learning materials, published by
BPP Learning Media Ltd, are printed on
paper obtained from traceable sustainable
sources.

The contents of this book are intended as a guide and not for professional advice. Although every effort has been made to ensure that the contents of this book are correct at the time of going to press, BPP Learning Media makes no warranty that the information in this book is accurate or complete and accepts no liability for any loss or damaged suffered by any person acting or refraining from acting as a result of the material in this book.

We are grateful to the AAT for permission to reproduce the sample assessment(s). The answers to the sample assessment(s) have been published by the AAT. All other answers have been prepared by BPP Learning Media Ltd.

BPP Learning Media is grateful to the IASB for permission to reproduce extracts from the International Financial Reporting Standards including all International Accounting Standards, SIC and IFRIC Interpretations (the Standards). The Standards together with their accompanying documents are issued by:

The International Accounting Standards Board (IASB) 30 Cannon Street, London, EC4M 6XH, United Kingdom. Email: info@ifrs.org Web: www.ifrs.org

Disclaimer: The IASB, the International Financial Reporting Standards (IFRS) Foundation, the authors and the publishers do not accept responsibility for any loss caused by acting or refraining from acting in reliance on the material in this publication, whether such loss is caused by negligence or otherwise to the maximum extent permitted by law.

A note about copyright

Dear Customer

What does the little © mean and why does it matter?

Your market-leading BPP books, course materials and e-learning materials do not write and update themselves. People write them on their own behalf or as employees of an organisation that invests in this activity. Copyright law protects their livelihoods. It does so by creating rights over the use of the content.

Breach of copyright is a form of theft – as well as being a criminal offence in some jurisdictions, it is potentially a serious breach of professional ethics.

With current technology, things might seem a bit hazy but, basically, without the express permission of BPP Learning Media:

- Photocopying our materials is a breach of copyright

- Scanning, ripcasting or conversion of our digital materials into different file formats, uploading them to facebook or e-mailing them to your friends is a breach of copyright

You can, of course, sell your books, in the form in which you have bought them – once you have finished with them. (Is this fair to your fellow students? We update for a reason.) Please note the e-products are sold on a single user licence basis: we do not supply 'unlock' codes to people who have bought them secondhand.

And what about outside the UK? BPP Learning Media strives to make our materials available at prices students can afford by local printing arrangements, pricing policies and partnerships which are clearly listed on our website. A tiny minority ignore this and indulge in criminal activity by illegally photocopying our material or supporting organisations that do. If they act illegally and unethically in one area, can you really trust them?

Copyright © IFRS Foundation

CONTENTS

INTRODUCTION

This is BPP Learning Media's AAT Question Bank for *Final Accounts Preparation*. It is part of a suite of ground-breaking resources produced by BPP Learning Media for AAT assessments.

This Question Bank has been written in conjunction with the BPP Course Book, and has been carefully designed to enable students to practise all of the learning outcomes and assessment criteria for the units that make up *Final Accounts Preparation.* It is fully up to date as at April 2016 and reflects both the AAT's qualification specification and the sample assessment provided by the AAT.

This Question Bank contains these key features:

- Tasks corresponding to each chapter of the Course Book. Some tasks are designed for learning purposes, others are of assessment standard

- AAT's AQ2016 sample assessment and answers for *Final Accounts Preparation* and further BPP practice assessments

The emphasis in all tasks and assessments is on the practical application of the skills acquired.

VAT

You may find tasks throughout this Question Bank that need you to calculate or be aware of a rate of VAT. This is stated at 20% in these examples and questions.

Approaching the assessment

When you sit the assessment it is very important that you follow the on screen instructions. This means you need to carefully read the instructions, both on the introduction screens and during specific tasks.

When you access the assessment you should be presented with an introductory screen with information similar to that shown below (taken from the introductory screen from one of the AAT's AQ2016 Sample Assessments for *Final Accounts Preparation*.

We have provided this **sample assessment** to help you familiarise yourself with our e-assessment environment. It is designed to demonstrate as many as possible of the question types that you may find in a live assessment. It is not designed to be used on its own to determine whether you are ready for a live assessment.

Assessment information:

You have **2 hours** to complete this sample assessment.

This assessment contains **6 tasks** and you should attempt to complete **every** task.
Each task is independent. You will not need to refer to your answers to previous tasks.
Read every task carefully to make sure you understand what is required.

The standard rate of VAT is 20%.

Where the date is relevant, it is given in the task data.
Both minus signs and brackets can be used to indicate negative numbers **unless** task instructions say otherwise.

You must use a full stop to indicate a decimal point. For example, write 100.57 NOT 100,57 or 100 57
You may use a comma to indicate a number in the thousands, but you don't have to. For example 10000 and 10,000 are both acceptable.

Copyright © 2016 AAT
All rights reserved. Reproduction is permitted for personal and educational use only. No part of this content may be reproduced or transmitted for commercial use without the copyright holder's written consent.

The actual instructions will vary depending on the subject you are studying for. It is very important you read the instructions on the introductory screen and apply them in the assessment. You don't want to lose marks when you know the correct answer just because you have not entered it in the right format.

In general, the rules set out in the AAT Sample Assessments for the subject you are studying for will apply in the real assessment, but you should carefully read the information on this screen again in the real assessment, just to make sure. This screen may also confirm the VAT rate used if applicable.

A full stop is needed to indicate a decimal point. We would recommend using minus signs to indicate negative numbers and leaving out the comma signs to indicate thousands, as this results in a lower number of key strokes and less margin for error when working under time pressure. Having said that, you can use whatever is easiest for you as long as you operate within the rules set out for your particular assessment.

You have to show competence throughout the assessment and you should therefore complete all of the tasks. Don't leave questions unanswered.

In some assessments, written or complex tasks may be human marked. In this case you are given a blank space or table to enter your answer into. You are told in the assessments which tasks these are (note: there may be none if all answers are marked by the computer).

If these involve calculations, it is a good idea to decide in advance how you are going to lay out your answers to such tasks by practising answering them on a word document, and certainly you should try all such tasks in this Question Bank and in the AAT's environment using the sample assessment.

When asked to fill in tables, or gaps, never leave any blank even if you are unsure of the answer. Fill in your best estimate.

Note that for some assessments where there is a lot of scenario information or tables of data provided (eg tax tables), you may need to access these via 'pop-ups'. Instructions will be provided on how you can bring up the necessary data during the assessment.

Finally, take note of any task specific instructions once you are in the assessment. For example you may be asked to enter a date in a certain format or to enter a number to a certain number of decimal places.

Grading

To achieve the qualification and to be awarded a grade, you must pass all the mandatory unit assessments, all optional unit assessments (where applicable) and the synoptic assessment.

The AAT Level 3 Advanced Diploma in Accounting will be awarded a grade. This grade will be based on performance across the qualification. Unit assessments and synoptic assessments are not individually graded. These assessments are given a mark that is used in calculating the overall grade.

How overall grade is determined

You will be awarded an overall qualification grade (Distinction, Merit, and Pass). If you do not achieve the qualification you will not receive a qualification certificate, and the grade will be shown as unclassified.

The marks of each assessment will be converted into a percentage mark and rounded up or down to the nearest whole number. This percentage mark is then weighted according to the weighting of the unit assessment or synoptic assessment within the qualification. The resulting weighted assessment percentages are combined to arrive at a percentage mark for the whole qualification.

Grade definition	Percentage threshold
Distinction	90–100%
Merit	80–89%
Pass	70–79%
Unclassified	0–69% Or failure to pass one or more assessment/s

Re-sits

Some AAT qualifications such as the AAT Advanced Diploma in Accounting have restrictions in place for how many times you are able to re-sit assessments. Please refer to the AAT website for further details.

You should only be entered for an assessment when you are well prepared and you expect to pass the assessment.

AAT qualifications

The material in this book may support the following AAT qualifications:

AAT Advanced Diploma in Accounting Level 3, AAT Advanced Diploma in Accounting at SCQF Level 6 and Further Education and Training Certificate: Accounting Technician (Level 4 AATSA)

Supplements

From time to time we may need to publish supplementary materials to one of our titles. This can be for a variety of reasons. From a small change in the AAT unit guidance to new legislation coming into effect between editions.

You should check our supplements page regularly for anything that may affect your learning materials. All supplements are available free of charge on our supplements page on our website at:

www.bpp.com/learning-media/about/students

Improving material and removing errors

There is a constant need to update and enhance our study materials in line with both regulatory changes and new insights into the assessments.

From our team of authors BPP appoints a subject expert to update and improve these materials for each new edition.

Their updated draft is subsequently technically checked by another author and from time to time non-technically checked by a proof reader.

We are very keen to remove as many numerical errors and narrative typos as we can but given the volume of detailed information being changed in a short space of time we know that a few errors will sometimes get though our net.

We apologise in advance for any inconvenience that an error might cause. We continue to look for new ways to improve these study materials and would welcome your suggestions. If you have any comments about this book, please email nisarahmed@bpp.com or write to Nisar Ahmed, AAT Head of Programme, BPP Learning Media Ltd, BPP House, Aldine Place, London W12 8AA.

Question bank

Chapter 1 – Organisations and their financial accounts

Task 1.1

Indicate with a tick whether each of the following balances is an asset, a liability, income, an expense or capital.

Balance	Asset ✓	Liability ✓	Income ✓	Expense ✓	Capital ✓
Salaries					
Bank overdraft					
Office costs					
Bank loan					
Capital					
Receivables					
Purchases					
Discount received					

Task 1.2

Given below is a trial balance for a business. Indicate with a tick as to whether each item in the trial balance falls into the category of asset, liability, income, expense or capital.

Balance	Debit £	Credit £	Asset ✓	Liability ✓	Income ✓	Expense ✓	Capital ✓
Rent cost	11,400						
Sales		143,000					
Opening inventory	2,400						
Payables		6,000					
Purchases	86,200						
Drawings	17,910						
Telephone costs	1,250						
Discounts received		80					
Distribution costs	400						
Motor vehicles	32,600						
Receivables	11,900						
Discounts allowed	120						
Capital		40,000					
Wages	20,600						
Heat and light	1,600						
Computer	2,400						
Bank	300						
	189,080	189,080					

Task 1.3

A business has made sales during the year of £867,450. The opening inventory of goods was £24,578 and the closing inventory was £30,574. During the year there were purchases made of £426,489. Distribution costs for the year were £104,366 and administration expenses totalled £87,689.

What are the gross profit and profit for the year?

Gross profit	£	
Profit for the year	£	

....

Task 1.4

What are the main categories of items that appear on a statement of financial position for a business?

....

Task 1.5

Decide whether each of the following balances would be an asset or liability on the statement of financial position or an item of income or expense in profit or loss. For the statement of financial position items indicate what types of asset or liability they are.

Balance	Asset ✓	Liability ✓	Income ✓	Expense ✓	Type of asset/liability
A company car					
Interest on a bank overdraft					
A bank loan repayable in five years					
Petty cash of £25					
The portion of rent paid covering the period after the statement of financial position date					
Freehold property					
Payment of wages for a manager with a two year service contract					
An irrecoverable debt written off					

....

Task 1.6

Describe the form and function of the statement of financial position and the statement of profit or loss.

Statement of financial position (SFP)

Statement of profit or loss (P/L)

Task 1.7

Classify the following items as long-term assets ('non-current assets'), short-term assets ('current assets') or liabilities.

Classification	Non-current assets ✓	Current assets ✓	Liabilities ✓
A PC used in the accounts department of a shop			
A PC on sale in an office equipment shop			
Wages due to be paid to staff at the end of the week			
A van for sale in a motor dealer's showroom			
A delivery van used in a grocer's business			
An amount owing to a bank for a loan for the acquisition of a van, to be repaid over 9 months			

Task 1.8

Fill in the missing words:

The trading account shows the [   ] profit for the period.

The bottom line of the statement of profit or loss shows the [   ] .

Task 1.9

	Yes ✓	No ✓
Is a bank overdraft a current liability?		

Chapter 2 – Incomplete records

Task 2.1

On 1 January 20X8, a business had assets of £10,000 and liabilities of £7,000. By 31 December 20X8 it had assets of £15,000 and liabilities of £10,000. The owner had contributed capital of £4,000.

Use the T account below to calculate how much profit or loss the business had made over the year.

£	

Capital account

	£		£

Task 2.2

The net assets of a business totalled £14,689 at 1 January 20X8 and £19,509 at 31 December 20X8. The owner did not pay any additional capital into the business but did withdraw £9,670 in drawings.

Use the T account below to calculate the profit or loss made by the business in the year.

£	

Capital account

	£		£

Task 2.3

A business has net assets of £31,240 on 31 May 20X8. On 1 June 20X7 the net assets of the business were £26,450. The owner knows that he took £12,300 of drawings out of the business during the year in cash and £560 of goods for his own use.

Use the T account below to calculate the profit or loss made by the business in the year.

£ [   ]

Capital account

	£		£

....

Task 2.4

A business had net assets at the start of the year of £23,695 and at the end of the year of £28,575. The business made a profit of £17,370 for the year.

Use the T account below to calculate the drawings made by the owner in the year.

£ [   ]

Capital account

	£		£

....

Task 2.5

The owner of a small shop provides you with the following information about its transactions for the month of May 20X8:

	£
Till rolls showing amounts paid into till	5,430
Paying in slip stub showing amount paid into bank from till	4,820
Cheques to payables totalling	3,980

The till always has a £100 cash float and the balance on the bank account at 1 May was £368 and at 31 May was £414. The owner has taken cash drawings out of the till and out of the bank account directly.

Use the T accounts below to calculate the drawings made by the owner in the month.

£	

Cash account

	£		£

Bank account

	£		£

Task 2.6

A small shop keeps a cash float of £250 in the till. The bank statement for the month of March 20X9 shows that the amount of cash paid into the bank for the month was £7,236. The owner keeps a record of the amounts of cash paid directly out of the till and knows that these consisted of wages of £320, cleaning costs of £50 and drawings of £1,050.

Use the T account below to calculate the sales in the month.

£ [   ]

Cash account

	£		£

Task 2.7

A business has a balance on its receivables account of £1,589 at the start of October 20X8 and this has risen to £2,021 by the end of October. The paying in slips for the month show that £5,056 was received from receivables during the month and discounts of £127 were allowed.

Use the T account below to calculate the credit sales in the month.

£ [   ]

Receivables account

	£		£

Task 2.8

The balance on a business's payables account at 1 March 20X9 was £4,266 and by 31 March was £5,111. During the month cheques paid to payables totalled £24,589 and discounts received were £491.

Use the T account below to calculate the credit purchases in the month.

£	

Payables account

	£		£
	_____		_____
	=======		=======

Task 2.9

A shop operates with a mark-up on cost of 20%. The purchases for the month of May totalled £3,600 and the inventory at the start of May was £640 and at the end of May was £570.

What were the sales for the month?

£	

Task 2.10

A shop operates with a mark-up on cost of 30%. The sales for the period were £5,200 and the inventory at the start and end of the period were £300 and £500.

What were the purchases for the period?

£	

Task 2.11

A shop operates on the basis of a profit margin of 20%. The purchases for the month of April totalled £5,010 and the inventory at the start and the end of the month was £670 and £980 respectively.

What are the sales for the period?

£ [   ]

··

Task 2.12

Sheena Gordon has been trading for just over 12 months as a dressmaker. She has kept no accounting records at all, and she is worried that she may need professional help to sort out her financial position, and she has approached you.

You meet with Sheena Gordon and discuss the information that you require her to give you. Sometime later, you receive a letter from Sheena Gordon providing you with the information that you requested, as follows:

(i) She started her business on 1 October 20X7. She opened a business bank account and paid in £5,000 of her savings.

(ii) During October she bought the equipment and the inventory of materials that she needed. The equipment cost £4,000 and the inventory of materials cost £1,800. All of this was paid for out of the business bank account.

(iii) A summary of the business bank account for the twelve months ended 30 September 20X8 showed the following.

	£		£
Capital	5,000	Equipment	4,000
Cash banked	27,000	Opening inventory of materials	1,800
		Purchases of materials	18,450
		General expenses	870
		Drawings	6,200
		Balance c/d	680
	32,000		32,000

(iv) All of the sales are on a cash basis. Some of the cash is paid into the bank account while the rest is used for cash expenses. She has no idea what the total value of her sales is for the year, but she knows that she has spent £3,800 on materials and £490 on general expenses. She took the rest of the cash not banked for her private drawings. She also keeps a cash float of £100.

(v) The gross profit margin on all sales is 50%.

(vi) She estimates that all the equipment should last for five years. You therefore agree to depreciate it using the straight-line method.

(vii) On 30 September 20X8, the payables for materials amounted to £1,400.

(viii) She estimates that the cost of inventory of materials that she had left at the end of the year was £2,200.

You are required to:

(a) **Calculate the total purchases for the year ended 30 September 20X8**

£ [ ]

(b) **Calculate the total cost of sales for the year ended 30 September 20X8**

£ [ ]

(c) **Calculate the sales for the year ended 30 September 20X8**

£ [ ]

(d) **Show the entries that would appear in Sheena Gordon's cash account**

Cash account

	£		£

(e) **Calculate the total drawings made by Sheena Gordon throughout the year**

£ [ ]

(f) **Calculate the figure for profit for the year ended 30 September 20X8**

£ [ ]

Task 2.13

(a) At 1 January 20X1 suppliers were owed £10,000, by 31 December 20X1 they were owed £8,000. In the year, receivables and payables contras were £3,500, and £350 of debit balances were transferred to receivables. Credit purchases were £60,000 and £2,500 of discounts were received.

What was paid to suppliers during the year?

	✓
£55,650	
£56,000	
£56,350	
£58,000	

(b) A business has opening inventory of £30,000 and achieves a mark-up of 25% on cost. Sales totalled £1,000,000, purchases were £840,000.

Calculate closing inventory.

	✓
£30,000	
£40,000	
£120,000	
£70,000	

Task 2.14

A sole trader has net assets of £19,000 at 30 April 20X9. During the year to 30 April 20X9 he introduced £9,800 additional capital into the business. Profits were £8,000, of which he withdrew £4,200.

His capital at 1 May 20X8 was:

✓	
	£3,000
	£5,400
	£13,000
	£16,600

Chapter 3 – Accounts for sole traders

Task 3.1

A sole trader had a capital balance of £32,569 on 1 May 20X8. During the year ended 30 April 20X9 the business made a profit for the year of £67,458 and the owner withdrew cash totalling £35,480 and goods with a cost of £1,680.

What is the capital balance at 30 April 20X9?

£ [   ]

Task 3.2

A sole trader took goods from his business with a cost of £560 for his own personal use.

What is the double entry for this transaction?

Debit	with £560
Credit	with £560

Task 3.3

The draft trial balance for a sole trader for the year ended 30 June is as follows:

	£
Machinery at cost	140,000
Motor vehicles at cost	68,000
Furniture and fittings at cost	23,000
Accumulated depreciation – machinery	64,500
Accumulated depreciation – motor vehicles	31,200
Accumulated depreciation – furniture and fittings	13,400

The depreciation charges for the year to 30 June have not yet been accounted for and the sole trader's depreciation policies are:

Machinery	20% on cost
Motor vehicles	35% diminishing balance
Furniture and fittings	20% diminishing balance

What is the total carrying amount of the non-current assets that will appear in the statement of financial position at 30 June?

£ [   ]

Task 3.4

A sole trader has produced the following final trial balance:

Trial balance at 31 May 20X8

	Debit £	Credit £
Bank		1,650
Capital		74,000
Payables		40,800
Receivables	60,000	
Discounts allowed	2,950	
Discounts received		2,000
Drawings	30,000	
Furniture and fittings at cost	24,500	
Electricity	2,950	
Insurance	2,300	
Miscellaneous expenses	1,500	
Motor expenses	3,100	
Motor vehicles at cost	48,000	
Purchases	245,000	
Allowance for doubtful debts		1,200
Accumulated depreciation – furniture and fittings		8,550
– motor vehicles		29,800
Rent	3,400	
Sales		369,000
Opening inventory	41,000	
Telephone costs	1,950	
VAT		4,100
Wages	52,000	
Closing inventory	43,500	43,500
Depreciation expense – furniture and fittings	2,450	
Depreciation expense – motor vehicles	7,800	
Irrecoverable debts expense	1,700	
Accruals		1,000
Prepayments	1,500	
	575,600	575,600

Prepare the financial statements for the year ended 31 May 20X8.

Statement of profit or loss for the year ended 31 May 20X8

	£	£
Sales revenue		
Cost of goods sold		
Gross profit		
Total expenses		
Profit/(loss) for the year		

Statement of financial position as at 31 May 20X8

	Cost	Depreciation	Carrying amount
	£	£	£
Non-current assets			
Current assets			
Current liabilities			
Net current assets			
Net assets			
Financed by:			

Task 3.5

Given below is the final trial balance of a sole trader for his year ended 30 June 20X8.

Final trial balance as at 30 June 20X8

	£	£
Administration expenses	7,490	
Bank	2,940	
Capital		60,000
Payables		20,200
Receivables	14,000	
Discounts allowed	2,510	
Discounts received		2,550
Distribution costs	1,530	
Drawings	14,600	
Machinery at cost	58,400	
Motor vehicles at cost	22,100	
Office costs	1,570	
Cost of goods sold	118,400	
Allowance for doubtful debts		280
Accumulated depreciation		
– Machinery		35,040
– Motor vehicles		12,785
Sales		167,400
Selling expenses	6,140	
VAT		3,690
Wages	16,700	
Closing inventory	18,200	
Irrecoverable debts expense	2,820	
Accruals		680
Prepayments	440	
Depreciation expense – machinery	11,680	
Depreciation expense – motor vehicles	3,105	
	302,625	302,625

Prepare the financial statements of the sole trader for the year ended 30 June 20X8.

Statement of profit or loss for the year ended 30 June 20X8

	£	£
Sales revenue		
Cost of goods sold		
Gross profit		
Total expenses		
Profit/(loss) for the year		

Statement of financial position as at 30 June 20X8

	Cost £	Depreciation £	Carrying amount £
Non-current assets			
Machinery	58 000	35 300	22 700
MV		12 915	19 915
Current assets			
	35 300		35
Current liabilities			
Net current assets			
Net assets			
Financed by:			

Task 3.6

A sole trader has prepared his financial statements from his trial balance. Extracts from that trial balance are given below:

	£	£
Sales		184,321
Purchases	91,201	
General expenses	16,422	

You are required to prepare journal entries showing how these accounts would be closed off at the year end.

	Debit	Credit
	£	£

Task 3.7

A trial balance contains the following balances:

	£
Opening inventory	2,000
Closing inventory	4,000
Purchases	20,000
Purchases returns	400
Settlement discounts received	1,600

What is the cost of sales?

£ _____

Task 3.8

For a statement of financial position to balance, identify with a tick which of the following statements is wrong?

✓	
	Net assets = owner's funds
	Net assets = capital + profit + drawings
	Net assets = capital + profit – drawings
	Non-current assets + net current assets = capital + profit – drawings

Chapter 4 – Accounts for partnerships

Task 4.1

Jim, Rob and Fiona are in partnership sharing profits in the ratio of 4 : 3 : 2. At 1 January 20X8 the balances on their current accounts were:

Jim	£2,000
Rob	£1,000 (debit)
Fiona	£3,500

During the year to 31 December 20X8 the partnership made a profit of £135,000 and the partners' drawings during the year were:

Jim	£58,000
Rob	£40,000
Fiona	£32,000

Write up the partners' current accounts for the year ended 31 December 20X8. Show the balance b/d on 1 January 20X9.

Current account – Jim

	£		£

Current account – Rob

	£		£

Current account – Fiona

	£		£

Task 4.2

Josh and Ken are in partnership sharing profits in a ratio of 2 : 1. Ken is allowed a salary of £8,000 per annum and both partners receive interest on their capital balances at 3% per annum. An extract from their trial balance at 30 June 20X8 is given below.

		£
Capital	Josh	40,000
	Ken	25,000
Drawings	Josh	21,000
	Ken	17,400
Current account (credit balances)	Josh	1,300
	Ken	800

The partnership made a profit for the year ended 30 June 20X8 of £39,950.

Write up the profit appropriation account and the partners' current accounts and show the balances that would appear in the statement of financial position for the capital accounts and current accounts.

Profit appropriation account

	£		£

Current account – Josh

	£		£

Current account – Ken

	£		£

Statement of financial position balances

Task 4.3

Jo, Emily and Karen are in partnership sharing profits equally. Emily is allowed a salary of £4,000 per annum and all partners receive interest on their capital balances at 5% per annum.

Given below is the final trial balance of the partnership between Jo, Emily and Karen at 30 June 20X8.

Final trial balance

	Debit £	Credit £
Advertising	3,140	
Bank	1,400	
Capital Jo		25,000
Emily		15,000
Karen		10,000
Payables		33,100
Current accounts Jo		1,000
Emily		540
Karen		230
Receivables	50,000	
Drawings Jo	12,000	
Emily	10,000	
Karen	10,000	
Electricity	4,260	
Furniture and fittings at cost	12,500	
Furniture and fittings – accumulated depreciation		7,025
Insurance	1,800	
Machinery at cost	38,000	
Machinery – accumulated depreciation		23,300
Allowance for doubtful debts		1,500
Cost of goods sold	198,300	
Sales		306,000
Sundry expenses	2,480	
Telephone expenses	2,150	
VAT		1,910
Wages	43,200	
Inventory at 30 June 20X8	24,100	
Depreciation expense – machinery	7,600	
Depreciation expense – furniture and fittings	1,825	
Irrecoverable debts expense	1,550	
Accruals		400
Prepayments	700	
	425,005	425,005

You are required to:

(a) **Prepare the statement of profit or loss for the year ended 30 June 20X8**

(b) **Write up the profit appropriation account and partners' current accounts showing their share of profits and their drawings. Show the balance b/d on 1 July 20X8.**

(c) **Prepare the statement of financial position as at 30 June 20X8**

(a) **Statement of profit or loss for the year ended 30 June 20X8**

	£	£
Sales revenue		
Cost of goods sold		
Gross profit		
Total expenses		
Profit/(loss) for the year		

(b) **Appropriation of profit**

		£	£
Profit for the year			
Profit available for distribution			
Profit share			

Current account – Jo

	£		£

Current account – Emily

	£		£

Current account – Karen

	£		£

(c) **Statement of financial position as at 30 June 20X8**

	Cost	Depreciation	Carrying amount
	£	£	£
Non-current assets			
Current assets			
Current liabilities			
Net current assets			
Net assets			
Financed by:			

Task 4.4

Ian and Max have been in partnership for a number of years sharing profits in the ratio of 2 : 1. The net assets of the partnership total £145,000 and it is believed that in addition the partnership has goodwill of £18,000. Len is to be admitted to the partnership on 1 June 20X8 and is to pay in £32,600 of capital. After Len has been admitted the profits will be shared 2 : 2 : 1.

Write up the partners' capital accounts given below to reflect the goodwill adjustment and the admission of the new partner.

Capital accounts

	Ian £	Max £	Len £		Ian £	Max £	Len £
				Bal b/d	85,000	60,000	
Good							

Task 4.5

Theo, Deb and Fran have been in partnership for a number of years but on 31 December 20X8 Deb is to retire. The credit balances on the partners' capital and current accounts at that date are:

		£
Capital	Theo	84,000
	Deb	62,000
	Fran	37,000
Current	Theo	4,500
	Deb	1,300
	Fran	6,200

Before the retirement of Deb the partners had shared profits in the ratio of 3 : 2 : 1. However after Deb's retirement the profit sharing ratio between Theo and Fran is to be 2 : 1. The goodwill of the partnership on 31 December 20X8 is estimated to be £54,000. The agreement with Deb is that she will be paid £10,000 at the date of retirement and the remainder of the amount that is due to her will take the form of a loan to the partnership.

Write up the partners' capital and current accounts to reflect Deb's retirement.

Capital accounts

	Theo £	Deb £	Fran £		Theo £	Deb £	Fran £
good	36,000			goodwill			
Bank		10,000				1,300	
loan		11,500					
bcd	73,000		28,000				
	11,000		45,000				

Current accounts

	Theo	Deb	Fran		Theo	Deb	Fran
	£	£	£		£	£	£

....

Task 4.6

During the year to 30 September 20X8 the partnership of Will and Clare Evans made a profit for the year of £90,000. From 1 October 20X7 until 30 June 20X8 the partnership agreement was as follows:

		Per annum
		£
Salaries	Will	10,000
	Clare	15,000

Interest on capital 3% of the opening capital balance

Profit share	Will	two-thirds
	Clare	one-third

However on 1 July 20X8 the partnership agreement was changed as follows:

		£
Salaries	Will	12,000
	Clare	20,000

Interest on capital 3% of the opening capital balance

Profit share	Will	three-quarters
	Clare	one-quarter

The opening balances at 1 October 20X7 on their capital and current accounts were as follows:

		£
Capital	Will	80,000
	Clare	50,000
Current	Will	2,000 (credit)
	Clare	3,000 (debit)

During the year ended 30 September 20X8 Will made drawings of £44,000 and Clare made drawings of £37,000.

At 30 June 20X8 the goodwill in the partnership was valued at £60,000. The partners have agreed that goodwill should be reallocated following the change to the partnership agreement.

Prepare the partnership profit appropriation account and the partners' current and capital accounts for the year ended 30 September 20X8.

Profit appropriation account

	1 October 20X7 to 30 June 20X8	1 July 20X8 to 30 Sept 20X8	Total
	£	£	£
Profit for distribution			
Profit share			

Current accounts

	Will	Clare		Will	Clare
	£	£		£	£

Capital accounts

	Will	Clare		Will	Clare
	£	£		£	£

Task 4.7

Mary Rose, Nelson Victory and Elizabeth Second are in partnership together hiring out river boats. Mary has decided to retire from the partnership at the end of the day on 31 March 20X9. You have been asked to finalise the partnership accounts for the year ended 31 March 20X9 and to make the entries necessary to account for the retirement of Mary from the partnership on that day.

You have been given the following information:

1   The profit for the year ended 31 March 20X9 was £106,120.

2   The partners are entitled to the following salaries per annum.

	£
Mary	18,000
Nelson	16,000
Elizabeth	13,000

3   Interest on capital is to be paid at a rate of 12% on the balance at the beginning of the year on the capital accounts. No interest is paid on the current accounts.

4   Cash drawings in the year amounted to:

	£
Mary	38,000
Nelson	30,000
Elizabeth	29,000

5   The balances on the current and capital accounts at 1 April 20X8 were as follows.

Capital accounts	£	Current accounts	£
Mary	28,000 (credit)	Mary	2,500 (credit)
Nelson	26,000 (credit)	Nelson	2,160 (credit)
Elizabeth	22,000 (credit)	Elizabeth	1,870 (credit)

6   The profit-sharing ratios in the partnership are currently:

Mary	4/10
Nelson	3/10
Elizabeth	3/10

On the retirement of Mary, Nelson will put a further £40,000 of capital into the business. The new profit-sharing ratios will be:

Nelson	6/10
Elizabeth	4/10

7   The goodwill in the partnership is to be valued at £90,000 on 31 March 20X9. No separate account for goodwill is to be maintained in the books of the partnership. Any adjusting entries in respect of goodwill are to be made in the capital accounts of the partners.

8   Any amounts to the credit of Mary on the date of her retirement should be transferred to a loan account.

You are required to:

(a) **Prepare the partners' capital accounts as at 31 March 20X9 showing the adjustments that need to be made on the retirement of Mary from the partnership**

(b) **Prepare an appropriation account for the partnership for the year ended 31 March 20X9**

(c) **Prepare the partners' current accounts for the year ended 31 March 20X9**

(d) **Show the balance on Mary's loan account as at 31 March 20X9**

(a) **Partners' capital accounts**

Partners' capital accounts

	Mary £	Nelson £	Elizabeth £		Mary £	Nelson £	Elizabeth £

(b) **Mary, Nelson and Elizabeth**

Profit appropriation account for the year ended 31 March 20X9

	£	£
Profit for the year		106,120
Profit available for distribution		
Profit share		

(c)

Partners' current accounts

	Mary	Nelson	Elizabeth		Mary	Nelson	Elizabeth
	£	£	£		£	£	£

(d)

Mary: loan account

	£		£

Task 4.8

Fill in the missing word regarding the definition of a partnership.

A partnership is a relationship between persons carrying on a business in common with a view to [   ] .

Task 4.9

What is the double entry for drawings made by a partner?

Debit	
Credit	

Task 4.10

What is the double entry to record interest earned on partners' capital account balances?

✓		
	Debit	partners' current accounts
	Credit	profit and loss appropriation account
	Debit	profit and loss appropriation account
	Credit	partners' current accounts
	Debit	profit and loss appropriation account
	Credit	cash
	Debit	profit and loss appropriation account
	Credit	partners' capital accounts

Task 4.11

You have the following information about a partnership:

The partners are Derek and Eva.

- Fabio was admitted to the partnership on 1 April 20X1 when he introduced £60,000 to the bank account.

- Profit share, effective until 31 March 20X1:

  - Derek   50%
  - Eva   50%

- Profit share, effective from 1 April 20X1:

  - Derek   40%
  - Eva   40%
  - Fabio   20%

- Goodwill was valued at £44,000 on 31 March 20X1.

- Goodwill is to be introduced into the partners' capital accounts on 31 March and then eliminated on 1 April.

(a) **Prepare the capital account for Fabio, the new partner, showing clearly the balance carried down as at 1 April 20X1.**

Capital account – Fabio

	£		£
		Balance b/d	0

(b) **Complete the following sentence by selecting the appropriate phrase from the picklist in each case:**

When a partner retires from a partnership business, the balance on the [▼] must be transferred to the [▼]

Picklist

business bank account
partner's capital account
partner's current account

Chapter 5 – Introduction to limited company accounts

Task 5.1

Computer software, although for long-term use in the business, is charged to the statement of profit or loss when purchased as its value is small in comparison with the hardware.

Which accounting concept determines this treatment?

Task 5.2

Explain each of the following four objectives which determine an organisation's choice of accounting policies.

Relevance

Reliability

Comparability

Ease of understanding

Task 5.3

Which of the following is not an accounting concept?

✓	
	Prudence
	Consistency
	Depreciation
	Accruals

Task 5.4

Which of the following standards provides guidance for property, plant and equipment, where IFRS is adopted?

✓	
	IAS 1
	IAS 6
	IAS 2
	IAS 16

Task 5.5

Which of the following standards provides guidance for inventories, where IFRS is adopted?

✓	
	IAS 2
	IAS 1
	IAS 16
	IAS 12

Answer bank

Chapter 1

Task 1.1

Balance	Asset ✓	Liability ✓	Income ✓	Expense ✓	Capital ✓
Salaries				✓	
Bank overdraft		✓			
Office costs				✓	
Bank loan		✓			
Capital					✓
Receivables	✓				
Purchases				✓	
Discount received			✓		

Task 1.2

Trial balance	Debit £	Credit £	Asset ✓	Liability ✓	Income ✓	Expense ✓	Capital ✓
Rent cost	11,400					✓	
Sales		143,000			✓		
Opening inventory	2,400					✓	
Payables		6,000		✓			
Purchases	86,200					✓	
Drawings	17,910						✓
Telephone costs	1,250					✓	
Discounts received		80			✓		
Distribution costs	400					✓	
Motor vehicles	32,600		✓				
Receivables	11,900		✓				
Discounts allowed	120					✓	
Capital		40,000					✓
Wages	20,600					✓	
Heat and light	1,600					✓	
Computer	2,400		✓				
Bank	300		✓				
	189,080	189,080					

Task 1.3

Gross profit	£	446,957
Profit for the year	£	254,902

Workings:

	£	£
Sales revenue		867,450
Cost of sales:		
Opening inventory	24,578	
Purchases	426,489	
	451,067	
Less: closing inventory	(30,574)	
		(420,493)
Gross profit		446,957
Distribution costs		(104,366)
Administration costs		(87,689)
Profit for the year		254,902

Task 1.4

- Non-current assets
- Current assets – inventories, receivables, bank and cash
- Current liabilities – payables
- Long term liabilities – loans
- Capital
- Profits earned
- Drawings

Task 1.5

Balance	Asset ✓	Liability ✓	Income ✓	Expense ✓	Type of asset/liability
A company car	✓				Non-current asset
Interest on a bank overdraft				✓	
A bank loan repayable in five years		✓			Long-term liability
Petty cash of £25	✓				Current asset
The portion of rent paid covering the period after the statement of financial position date	✓				Prepayment (current asset)
Freehold property	✓				Non-current asset
Payment of wages for a manager with a two year service contract				✓	
An irrecoverable debt written off				✓	

Task 1.6

Statement of financial position (SFP)

A statement of financial position (SFP) is a list of the assets, liabilities and capital of a business at a given moment. Assets are divided into non-current assets and current assets. Liabilities may be current or non-current (long term).

Statement of profit or loss (P/L)

A statement of profit or loss (P/L) matches the revenue earned in a period with the costs incurred in earning it. It is usual to distinguish between a gross profit (sales revenue less the cost of goods sold) and a profit for the year (being the gross profit less the expenses of selling, distribution, administration and so on).

Task 1.7

Classification	Non-current assets ✓	Current assets ✓	Liabilities ✓
A PC used in the accounts department of a shop	✓		
A PC on sale in an office equipment shop		✓	
Wages due to be paid to staff at the end of the week			✓
A van for sale in a motor dealer's showroom		✓	
A delivery van used in a grocer's business	✓		
An amount owing to a bank for a loan for the acquisition of a van, to be repaid over 9 months			✓

Task 1.8

The trading account shows the gross profit for the period.

The bottom line of the statement of profit or loss shows the profit or loss for the period.

Task 1.9

	Yes ✓	No ✓
Is a bank overdraft a current liability?	✓	

Chapter 2

Task 2.1

£	2,000 loss

Workings:

	£
Assets 1 January 20X8	10,000
Liabilities 1 January 20X8	7,000
Owner's capital at 1 January 20X8	3,000

	£
Assets 31 December 20X8	15,000
Liabilities 31 December 20X8	10,000
Owner's capital at 31 December 20X8	5,000

Capital account

	£		£
Drawings	0	Balance b/d	3,000
Loss (bal fig)	2,000		
Balance c/d	5,000	Capital introduced	4,000
	7,000		7,000

Task 2.2

£	14,490 profit

Workings:

Capital account

	£		£
Drawings	9,670	Balance b/d	14,689
Balance c/d	19,509	Profit (bal fig)	14,490
	29,179		29,179

Task 2.3

£	17,650 profit

Workings:

Capital account

	£		£
Drawings	12,860	Balance b/d	26,450
Balance c/d	31,240	Profit (bal fig)	17,650
	44,100		44,100

Task 2.4

£	12,490

Workings:

Capital account

	£		£
Drawings (bal fig)	12,490	Balance b/d	23,695
Balance c/d	28,575	Profit	17,370
	41,065		41,065

Task 2.5

£	1,404

Workings:

Cash account

	£		£
Balance b/d	100	Bankings	4,820
Sales	5,430	Drawings (bal fig)	610
		Balance c/d	100
	5,530		5,530

Bank account

	£		£
Balance b/d	368	Payables	3,980
Bankings	4,820	Drawings (bal fig)	794
		Balance c/d	414
	5,188		5,188

Total drawings	£
Cash	610
Bank	794
	1,404

Task 2.6

£	8,656

Workings:

Cash account

	£		£
Balance b/d	250	Bankings	7,236
Sales (bal fig)	8,656	Wages	320
		Cleaning costs	50
		Drawings	1,050
		Balance c/d	250
	8,906		8,906

Task 2.7

£	5,615

Workings:

Receivables account

	£		£
Balance b/d	1,589	Bank	5,056
Sales (bal fig)	5,615	Discount allowed	127
		Balance c/d	2,021
	7,204		7,204

Task 2.8

£	25,925

Workings:

Payables account

	£		£
Bank	24,589	Balance b/d	4,266
Discounts received	491	Purchases (bal fig)	25,925
Balance c/d	5,111		
	30,191		30,191

Task 2.9

£	4,404

Workings:

	£	%
Sales (bal fig)	4,404	120
Cost of sales (640 + 3,600 − 570)	3,670	100
Gross profit	734	20

. . . .

Task 2.10

£	4,200

Workings:

	£	£	%
Sales revenue		5,200	130
Cost of sales			
Opening inventory	300		
Purchases (bal fig)	4,200		
	4,500		
Less: closing inventory	(500)		
Cost of sales (5,200 × 100/130)		4,000	100
Gross profit		1,200	30

. . . .

Task 2.11

£	5,875

Workings:

	£	%
Sales (bal fig)	5,875	100
Cost of sales (670 + 5,010 − 980)	4,700	80
Gross profit	1,175	20

. . . .

Task 2.12

(a) | £ | 25,450 |

Workings:

	£
Opening inventory	1,800
Payments: bank	18,450
cash	3,800
Payables	1,400
Total purchases	25,450

(b) | £ | 23,250 |

Workings:

	£
Purchases (from (a))	25,450
Closing inventory	(2,200)
Total cost of sales	23,250

(c) | £ | 46,500 |

Workings:

	£
Cost of sales (from (b))	23,250
Total sales (× 2) (gross profit margin 50%)	46,500

(d)

Cash account

	£		£
Sales (from (c))	46,500	Bank account	27,000
		Materials	3,800
		General expenses	490
		Drawings	15,110
		(balancing figure)	
		Bal c/d (float)	100
	46,500		46,500

(e) | £ | 21,310 |

Workings:

	£
Bank account	6,200
Cash account (from (d))	15,110
Total drawings	21,310

(f)   £ | 21,090

Workings:

	£	£
Sales (from (c))		46,500
Cost of sales (from (b))		(23,250)
Gross profit		23,250
General expenses (870 + 490)	1,360	
Depreciation (4,000/5)	800	
		(2,160)
Profit for the year		21,090

··

Task 2.13

(a)

	✓
£55,650	
£56,000	⌐
£56,350	✓
£58,000	

Workings:

Payables control account

	£		£
Contra	3,500	Balance b/d	10,000
Discounts received	2,500	Transfers to receivables	350
Cash paid (bal fig)	56,350	Purchases	60,000
Balance c/d	8,000		
	70,350		70,350

(b)

	✓
£30,000	
£40,000	
£120,000	
£70,000	✓

Workings:

	£	%
Sales	1,000,000	125
Cost of sales	800,000	100
Opening inventory	30,000	
Purchases	840,000	
	870,000	
Closing inventory (bal fig)	(70,000)	
Cost of sales	800,000	

Task 2.14

✓	
	£3,000
✓	£5,400
	£13,000
	£16,600

Workings:

	£
Opening capital (balancing figure)	5,400
Capital introduced	9,800
Profits	8,000
	23,200
Drawings	(4,200)
Net assets	19,000

Chapter 3

Task 3.1

£	62,867

Workings:

	£
Opening capital	32,569
Profit for the year	67,458
	100,027
Less: drawings (35,480 + 1,680)	37,160
Closing capital	62,867

Task 3.2

Debit	Drawings
Credit	Purchases

Task 3.3

£	79,100

Workings:

Depreciation charges				
– machinery	=	£140,000 × 20%	=	£28,000
– motor vehicles	=	(£68,000 – 31,200) × 35%	=	£12,880
– furniture and fittings	=	(£23,000 – 13,400) × 20%	=	£1,920

	Cost	Accumulated depreciation	Carrying amount
	£	£	£
Machinery	140,000	92,500	47,500
Motor vehicles	68,000	44,080	23,920
Furniture and fittings	23,000	15,320	7,680
			79,100

Task 3.4

Statement of profit or loss for the year ended 31 May 20X8

	£	£
Sales revenue		369,000
Less: Cost of sales		
Opening inventory	41,000	
Purchases	245,000	
	286,000	
Less: closing inventory	(43,500)	
Cost of goods sold		(242,500)
Gross profit		126,500
Discounts received		2,000
		128,500
Less: Expenses		
Discounts allowed	2,950	
Electricity	2,950	
Insurance	2,300	
Miscellaneous expenses	1,500	
Motor expenses	3,100	
Rent	3,400	
Telephone costs	1,950	
Wages	52,000	
Depreciation furniture and fittings	2,450	
motor vehicles	7,800	
Irrecoverable debts	1,700	
Total expenses		(82,100)
Profit for the year		46,400

Statement of financial position as at 31 May 20X8

	Cost £	Depreciation £	Carrying amount £
Non-current assets			
Furniture and fittings	24,500	8,550	15,950
Motor vehicles	48,000	29,800	18,200
	72,500	38,350	34,150
Current assets			
Inventory		43,500	
Receivables	60,000		
Less: allowance	1,200		
		58,800	
Prepayments		1,500	
		103,800	
Current liabilities			
Payables	40,800		
Bank overdraft	1,650		
Accruals	1,000		
VAT	4,100		
		47,550	
Net current assets			56,250
Net assets			90,400
Financed by:			
Opening capital			74,000
Profit for the year			46,400
			120,400
Less: drawings			30,000
			90,400

Task 3.5

Statement of profit or loss for the year ended 30 June 20X8

	£	£
Sales revenue		167,400
Cost of goods sold		(118,400)
Gross profit		49,000
Discounts received		2,550
		51,550
Less: Expenses		
Administration expenses	7,490	
Distribution costs	1,530	
Discounts allowed	2,510	
Office costs	1,570	
Selling expenses	6,140	
Wages	16,700	
Irrecoverable debts	2,820	
Depreciation expense:		
machinery	11,680	
motor vehicles	3,105	
Total expenses		(53,545)
Loss for the year		(1,995)

Statement of financial position as at 30 June 20X8

	Cost	Depreciation	Carrying amount
	£	£	£
Non-current assets			
Machinery	58,400	35,040	23,360
Motor vehicles	22,100	12,785	9,315
	80,500	47,825	32,675
Current assets			
Inventory		18,200	
Receivables	14,000		
Less: allowance	(280)		
		13,720	
Prepayments		440	
Bank		2,940	
		35,300	
Current liabilities			
Payables	20,200		
Accruals	680		
VAT	3,690		
		24,570	
Net current assets			10,730
Net assets			43,405
Financed by:			
Capital			60,000
Loss for the year			(1,995)
			58,005
Less: drawings			(14,600)
			43,405

Task 3.6

	Debit	Credit
	£	£
Sales	184,321	
Profit or loss ledger account		184,321
Profit or loss ledger account	91,201	
Purchases		91,201
Profit or loss ledger account	16,422	
General expenses		16,422

Task 3.7

£	17,600

Workings:

	£
Purchases	20,000
Less: purchases returns	(400)
	19,600
Add: opening inventory	2,000
Less: closing inventory	(4,000)
Cost of sales	17,600

Task 3.8

✓	
	Net assets = owner's funds
✓	Net assets = capital + profit + drawings
	Net assets = capital + profit – drawings
	Non-current assets + net current assets = capital + profit – drawings

Drawings reduce capital, so they must be deducted.

Chapter 4

Task 4.1

Current account – Jim

	£		£
Drawings	58,000	Balance b/d	2,000
Balance c/d	4,000	Profit share (135,000 × 4/9)	60,000
	62,000		62,000
		Balance b/d	4,000

Current account – Rob

	£		£
Balance b/d	1,000	Profit share (135,000 × 3/9)	45,000
Drawings	40,000		
Balance c/d	4,000		
	45,000		45,000
		Balance b/d	4,000

Current account – Fiona

	£		£
Drawings	32,000	Balance b/d	3,500
Balance c/d	1,500	Profit share (135,000 × 2/9)	30,000
	33,500		33,500
		Balance b/d	1,500

Task 4.2

Profit appropriation account

	£		£
Salary – Ken	8,000	Profit for the year b/d	39,950
Interest			
Josh (40,000 × 3%)	1,200		
Ken (25,000 × 3%)	750		
Balance c/d	30,000		
	39,950		39,950
		Profit for distribution	30,000
Profit share			
Josh (30,000 × 2/3)	20,000		
Ken (30,000 × 1/3)	10,000		
	30,000		30,000

Current account – Josh

	£		£
Drawings	21,000	Balance b/d	1,300
Balance c/d	1,500	Profit share (1,200 + 20,000)	21,200
	22,500		22,500
		Balance b/d	1,500

Current account – Ken

	£		£
Drawings	17,400	Balance b/d	800
		Profit share	
Balance c/d	2,150	(8,000 + 750 + 10,000)	18,750
	19,550		19,550
		Balance b/d	2,150

Statement of financial position balances

Capital accounts:

– Josh	£40,000
– Ken	£25,000

Current accounts:

– Josh	£1,500
– Ken	£2,150

Task 4.3

(a) **Statement of profit or loss for the year ended 30 June 20X8**

	£	£
Sales revenue		306,000
Cost of goods sold		(198,300)
Gross profit		107,700
Less: Expenses		
Advertising	3,140	
Electricity	4,260	
Insurance	1,800	
Sundry expenses	2,480	
Telephone expenses	2,150	
Wages	43,200	
Depreciation machinery	7,600	
furniture and fittings	1,825	
Irrecoverable debts	1,550	
Total expenses		(68,005)
Profit for the year		39,695

(b) **Appropriation of profit**

	£	£
Profit for the year		39,695
Salary – Emily		(4,000)
Interest Jo (25,000 × 5%)		(1,250)
Emily (15,000 × 5%)		(750)
Karen (10,000 × 5%)		(500)
Profit available for distribution		33,195
Profit share (33,195/3)		
Jo		11,065
Emily		11,065
Karen		11,065
		33,195

Current account – Jo

	£		£
Drawings	12,000	Bal b/d	1,000
Bal c/d	1,315	Interest	1,250
		Profit	11,065
	13,315		13,315
		Bal b/d	1,315

Current account – Emily

	£		£
Drawings	10,000	Bal b/d	540
Bal c/d	6,355	Salary	4,000
		Interest	750
		Profit	11,065
	16,355		16,355
		Bal b/d	6,355

Current account – Karen

	£		£
Drawings	10,000	Bal b/d	230
Bal c/d	1,795	Interest	500
		Profit	11,065
	11,795		11,795
		Bal b/d	1,795

(c) **Statement of financial position as at 30 June 20X8**

	Cost	Accumulated depreciation	Carrying amount
	£	£	£
Non-current assets			
Machinery	38,000	23,300	14,700
Furniture and fittings	12,500	7,025	5,475
	50,500	30,325	20,175
Current assets			
Inventory		24,100	
Receivables	50,000		
Less: allowance	1,500		
		48,500	
Prepayments		700	
Bank		1,400	
		74,700	
Current liabilities			
Payables	33,100		
Accruals	400		
VAT	1,910		
		35,410	
Net current assets			39,290
Net assets			59,465
Financed by:			
Capital accounts	Jo		25,000
	Emily		15,000
	Karen		10,000
			50,000
Current accounts	Jo	1,315	
	Emily	6,355	
	Karen	1,795	
			9,465
			59,465

Task 4.4

Capital accounts

	Ian £	Max £	Len £		Ian £	Max £	Len £
				Bal b/d	85,000	60,000	
Goodwill	7,200	7,200	3,600	Goodwill	12,000	6,000	
Balance c/d	89,800	58,800	29,000	Bank			32,600
	97,000	66,000	32,600		97,000	66,000	32,600

Task 4.5

Capital accounts

	Theo £	Deb £	Fran £		Theo £	Deb £	Fran £
				Balance b/d	84,000	62,000	37,000
				Current a/c		1,300	
Goodwill	36,000		18,000	Goodwill	27,000	18,000	9,000
Bank		10,000					
Loan		71,300					
Balance c/d	75,000		28,000				
	111,000	81,300	46,000		111,000	81,300	46,000

Current accounts

	Theo £	Deb £	Fran £		Theo £	Deb £	Fran £
Capital a/c		1,300		Balance b/d	4,500	1,300	6,200
Balance c/d	4,500		6,200				
	4,500	1,300	6,200		4,500	1,300	6,200

Task 4.6

Profit appropriation account

	1 October 20X7 to 30 June 20X8	1 July 20X8 to 30 Sept 20X8	Total
	£	£	£
Profit 9/12 and 3/12 × £90,000	67,500	22,500	90,000
Salaries			
Will (9/12 × 10,000) and (3/12 × 12,000)	(7,500)	(3,000)	(10,500)
Clare (9/12 × 15,000) and (3/12 × 20,000)	(11,250)	(5,000)	(16,250)
Interest			
Will 9/12 and 3/12 × £2,400	(1,800)	(600)	(2,400)
Clare 9/12 and 3/12 × £1,500	(1,125)	(375)	(1,500)
Profit for distribution	45,825	13,525	59,350
Profit share			
Will (2/3 × 45,825) and (3/4 × 13,525)	30,550	10,144	40,694
Clare (1/3 × 45,825) and (1/4 × 13,525)	15,275	3,381	18,656
	45,825	13,525	59,350

Current accounts

	Will	Clare		Will	Clare
	£	£		£	£
Balance b/d		3,000	Balance b/d	2,000	
Drawings	44,000	37,000	Salaries	10,500	16,250
Balance c/d	11,594		Interest	2,400	1,500
			Profit share	40,694	18,656
			Balance c/d		3,594
	55,594	40,000		55,594	40,000

Capital accounts

	Will	Clare		Will	Clare
	£	£		£	£
			Balance b/d	80,000	50,000
Goodwill	45,000	15,000	Goodwill	40,000	20,000
Balance c/d	75,000	55,000			
	120,000	70,000		120,000	70,000

Task 4.7

(a) **Partners' capital accounts**

Partners' capital accounts

	Mary	Nelson	Elizabeth		Mary	Nelson	Elizabeth
	£	£	£		£	£	£
Goodwill (6:4)	–	54,000	36,000	Balance b/d	28,000	26,000	22,000
Loan				Cash		40,000	
(bal. fig)	69,860	–	–	Goodwill (4:3:3)	36,000	27,000	27,000
Balance c/d	–	39,000	13,000	Current a/c	5,860		
	69,860	93,000	49,000		69,860	93,000	49,000

(b) **Mary, Nelson and Elizabeth**

Profit appropriation account for the year ended 31 March 20X9

	£	£
Profit for the year		106,120
Less: partners' salaries		
Mary	18,000	
Nelson	16,000	
Elizabeth	13,000	
		47,000
Less: interest on capital		
Mary (£28,000 × 12%)	3,360	
Nelson (£26,000 × 12%)	3,120	
Elizabeth (£22,000 × 12%)	2,640	
		9,120
Profit available for distribution		50,000
Profit share		
Mary 4/10		20,000
Nelson 3/10		15,000
Elizabeth 3/10		15,000
		50,000

(c)

Partners' current accounts

	Mary £	Nelson £	Elizabeth £		Mary £	Nelson £	Elizabeth £
Drawings	38,000	30,000	29,000	Balance b/d	2,500	2,160	1,870
Capital a/c	5,860	–	–	Interest on capital	3,360	3,120	2,640
Balance c/d	–	6,280	3,510	Salaries	18,000	16,000	13,000
				Profit	20,000	15,000	15,000
	43,860	36,280	32,510		43,860	36,280	32,510

(d)

Mary: loan account

	£		£
Balance c/d	69,860	Capital a/c	69,860
	69,860		69,860

Task 4.8

profit

Task 4.9

Debit	Current account
Credit	Bank or Purchases

Task 4.10

✓		
	Debit	partners' current accounts
	Credit	profit and loss appropriation account
✓	Debit	profit and loss appropriation account
	Credit	partners' current accounts
	Debit	profit and loss appropriation account
	Credit	cash
	Debit	profit and loss appropriation account
	Credit	partners' capital accounts

Interest on partners' capital is an appropriation of profit (debit appropriation account). Since partners have earned the money through their investment in the business, their current accounts should be credited with it.

Task 4.11

(a) **Capital account – Fabio**

	£		£
Goodwill	8,800	Balance b/d	0
Balance c/d	51,200	Bank	60,000
	60,000		60,000

(b) When a partner retires from a partnership business, the balance on the partner's current account must be transferred to the partner's capital account.

Chapter 5

Task 5.1

> Materiality

Task 5.2

> **Relevance**
>
> Financial information is said to be relevant if it has the ability to influence the economic decisions of the users of that information and is provided in time to influence those decisions. Where an organisation faces a choice of accounting policies they should choose the one that is more relevant in the context of the final accounts as a whole. Materiality also affects relevance.

> **Reliability**
>
> In the financial statements:
>
> - The figures should represent the substance of the transactions or events
>
> - The figures should be free from bias, or neutral
>
> - The figures should be free from material errors
>
> - A degree of caution should have been applied in making judgements where there is uncertainty

> **Comparability**
>
> Information in financial statements is used by many different people and organisations. It is much more useful to these users if it is comparable over time and also with similar information about other businesses. The selection of appropriate accounting policies and their consistent use should provide such comparability.

> **Ease of understanding**
>
> Accounting policies should be chosen to ensure ease of understanding for users of financial statements. For this purpose users are assumed to have a reasonable knowledge of business and economic activities and accounting and a willingness to study the information diligently.

Task 5.3

✓	
	Prudence
	Consistency
✓	Depreciation
	Accruals

Task 5.4

✓	
	IAS 1
	IAS 6
	IAS 2
✓	IAS 16

Task 5.5

✓	
✓	IAS 2
	IAS 1
	IAS 16
	IAS 12

Answer bank

AAT AQ2016 SAMPLE ASSESSMENT
FINAL ACCOUNTS PREPARATION

Time allowed: 2 hours

Final Accounts Preparation
AAT sample assessment

Task 1 (15 marks)

This task is about reconstructing general ledger accounts.

You are working on the accounting records of a sole trader for the year ended 31 March 20X7. The business is VAT registered.

You have the following information:

Daybook summaries:	Goods	VAT	Total
	£	£	£
Sales	159,100	31,820	190,920
Sales returns	1,610	322	1,932
Purchases	124,940	24,408	149,348
Purchases returns		None	

Further information:	Net	VAT	Total
	£	£	£
General expenses	7,510	1,502	9,012

Balances as at:	31 March 20X6	31 March 20X7
	£	£
Trade receivables	17,360	18,940
Trade payables	13,345	14,656
Closing inventory	10,520	11,300
VAT	1,806 credit	Not available
Bank	3,811 debit	Not available

- General expenses are not processed through the purchases daybook.
  £9,012 was posted to the general expenses account.
  All the VAT on these expenses is recoverable.

- Cash sales of £4,200 were made, excluding VAT at 20%
  The total banked was posted to the cash sales account.

- All purchases are on credit terms.

- The trader took advantage of settlement discounts whenever offered.

  VAT has been correctly accounted for.

Receipts and payments recorded in the bank account include:	£
Amounts from credit customers	187,408
Amounts to suppliers	145,137
Amounts banked from cash sales	5,040
Loan receipt	8,000
Rent paid	6,900
General expenses	9,012
HMRC for VAT – payment	6,169
Drawings	23,000
Wages	15,500

BPP
LEARNING MEDIA

(a) **Find the missing discounts figure by preparing the purchases ledger control account for the year ended 31 March 20X7.**

Purchases ledger control account

		£			£
	▼			▼	
	▼			▼	
	▼			▼	
	▼			▼	
		0			0

Drop-down list:

Balance b/d
Balance c/d
Bank
Cash purchases
Cash sales
Discounts allowed
Discounts received
Drawings
General ledger
Inventory
Loan
Purchases daybook
Rent
Sales daybook
Sales returns daybook
Wages

(b) **Find the closing balance on the VAT control account for the year ended 31 March 20X7.**

Note: The business is not charged VAT on its rent.

VAT control

		£			£
	▼			▼	
	▼			▼	
	▼			▼	
	▼			▼	
	▼			▼	
	▼			▼	
		0			0

Drop-down list:

Balance b/d
Balance c/d
Bank
Cash sales
Discounts allowed
Discounts received
Drawings
General expenses
General ledger
Inventory
Loan
Purchases daybook
Rent
Sales daybook
Sales returns daybook
Wages

The totals recorded in the cash book for the year ended 31 March 20X7 were:

Receipts   £200,448
Payments   £205,718

(c) **Assuming there are no year-end adjustments, what will be the opening bank account balance in the general ledger as at 1 April 20X7?**

£ [   ]   [▼]

Drop-down list:

Debit
Credit

....

Task 2 (15 marks)

This task is about incomplete records and applying ethical principles when preparing final accounts.

(a) **Show whether the following is TRUE or FALSE.**

Gross sales margin percentage may be calculated as: $\dfrac{\text{Gross profit}}{\text{Sales}} \times 100\%$

[ ] True

[ ] False

You are a trainee accounting technician who prepares final accounts for a number of sole trader clients.

You have the following information about a business for its year ended 31 March 20X7.

- It is not registered for VAT.
- The trader operates with a gross sales margin of 25%.
- Inventory at 1 April 20X6 was £5,050.
- Sales of £64,900 were made.
- Purchases were recorded as £48,390.

(b) **Using this information, complete the following tasks.**

    (i) **Calculate the cost of goods sold for the year ended 31 March 20X7.**

    £ [   ]

    (ii) **Calculate the value of closing inventory.**

    £ [   ]

You compare this figure with the results of a physical inventory count as at the year end. The total physical inventory value is £350 lower than your calculation above.

    (iii) **Which ONE of the following could explain this?**

    ☐ Some equipment used in the office was stolen during the year.

    ☐ There were unpaid sales invoices at the year end.

    ☐ A high value item was included twice in the count.

    ☐ The trader has made drawings of goods during the year.

    (iv) **Update the value of closing inventory to account for the difference above.**

    £ [   ]

The trader has a policy of allowing customers to settle their accounts one month after the sale is made.

(c) **Which of the following is most likely to be the total on the sales ledger at the end of the financial year?**

☐ £6,940

☐ £16,225

☐ £64,900

You are now working on the final accounts of another client.

Your manager is called away unexpectedly. He asks you to undertake a particular tasks with a deadline during his absence. You know you have not received sufficient training to do this work.

(d) **What should you do? Choose ONE.**

☐ Do the job to the best of your ability and submit the work to the client on time.

☐ Ask if you may have support from elsewhere in the organisation.

☐ Ask a family member who is a qualified accountant to do the work for you.

☐ Advise the client that the deadline will be missed.

Task 3 (18 marks)

This task is about final accounts for sole traders.

You have the following information about events on 1 January 20X7.

- A sole trader started business.
- The business was not registered for VAT.
- The sole trader transferred £13,000 of his own money to the business bank account.
- £1,100 was paid from this account for some office furniture.
- £900 of goods for resale were purchased. The supplier allowed one month of credit.

(a) **Complete the capital account as of 1 January 20X7, showing clearly the balance carried down.**

Capital

		£			£
	▼			▼	
	▼			▼	
	▼			▼	
		0			0

Drop-down list:

Balance b/d
Balance c/d
Bank
Drawings
Office furniture at cost
Purchases
Purchases ledger control account
Sales
Sales ledger control account
Suspense

e now working on the final accounts of another sole trader, Onyx Trading.

are to prepare the statement of financial position for Onyx Trading as at rch 20X7.

he final trial balance is below.

- profit for the year of £42,495 has been recorded.
- Onyx has a policy of showing trade receivables net of any allowance for doubtful debts.

(b) **Using this information, complete the following tasks:**

(i) **Calculate the value of trade receivables that will appear in the statement of financial position.**

£ [   ]

(ii) **Prepare the statement of financial position for Onyx Trading as at 31 March 20X7. Do NOT use brackets, minus signs or dashes.**

Onyx Trading

Trial balance as at 31 March 20X7

	DR £	CR £
Accruals		1,940
Administration expenses	33,193	
Advertising expenses	2,000	
Allowance for doubtful debts		1,200
Allowance for doubtful debts – adjustment	435	
Bank	1,645	
Bank charges	280	
Capital		22,200
Closing inventory	22,420	22,420
Depreciation charges	6,150	
Disposal of non-current assets		360
Drawings	20,000	
Equipment at cost	32,800	
Equipment accumulated depreciation		14,350
Opening inventory	20,720	
Payroll expenses	10,097	
Payroll liabilities		630
Prepayments	900	
Purchases	179,250	
Purchases ledger control account		16,720

	DR £	CR £
Rent	14,800	
Sales		287,340
Sales ledger control account	25,660	
Sales returns	700	
VAT		3,890
Total	371,050	371,050

Onyx Trading
Statement of financial position as at 31 March 20X7

	Cost £	Accumulated depreciation £	Carrying amount £
Non-current assets			
(1) ▼			
Current assets			
(1) ▼			
(1) ▼			
(1) ▼			
(1) ▼			
(1) ▼			
		0	
Current liabilities			
(1) ▼			
(1) ▼			
(1) ▼			
(1) ▼			
(1) ▼			
		0	
Net current assets			
Net assets			

	Cost £	Accumulated depreciation £	Carrying amount £
Financed by:			
Capital			
Opening capital			
(2) ▼			
(2) ▼			
Closing capital			

Drop-down list 1:

Accruals
Bank
Bank charges
Capital
Disposals
Drawings
Equipment
Expenses
Inventory
Payroll expenses
Payroll liabilities
Prepayments
Profit for the year
Purchases
Trade payables
Trade receivables
VAT

Drop-down list 2:

Add: Drawings
Add: Profit for the year
Less: Drawings
Less: Profit for the year

(c) **Complete the following:**

Drawings for the year will be transferred as a [▼] to the capital account in the general ledger.

The opening balance in the capital account on 1 April 20X7 will be: £ [ ]

Drop-down list:

debit
credit

Task 4 (16 marks)

This task is about the knowledge and understanding underpinning final accounts preparation.

(a) **Complete the following statements:**

(i) **Which ONE of the list below is a benefit of running a business as a sole trader?**

☐ Unlimited liability.

☐ Limited liability.

☐ Complete control over business decisions.

☐ No requirement to prepare annual accounts by a certain date.

(ii) **Complete the sentence:**

A private limited company is owned by its [▼]

Drop-down list:

directors.
shareholders.
trustees.

(iii) **Which of the following businesses have owners with limited liability for its debts?**

1. The Joe and Josephine Bloggs Partnership
2. Joe and Josephine Bloggs LLP
3. Joe Bloggs plc

☐ All of them

☐ 3 only

☐ 2 and 3

☐ 1 and 2

(iv) **Complete the following:**

To be a charity an organisation must satisfy the definition of a charity found in the

[▼]

Drop-down list:

Charities Act
Code of Practice for not for profit organisations

Its purpose must be for the benefit of the [▼]

Drop-down list:

public
trustees

(b) **Which ONE of the items below prescribes the format of final accounts for an organisation adopting IFRS?**

☐ IAS 1

☐ IAS 2

☐ IAS 2012

(c) **Link the boxes to match the following users of final accounts with the most likely reason for their interest. Make each selection by clicking on a box in the left column and then on one in the right column. You can remove a line by clicking on it.**

User	Reason
	Assessment of the security of any loan
Management	Decision making relating to their personal investment
Shareholders	To compare information from the other organisations operating within the same business sector
	To assess future performance of the business

Task 5 (15 marks)

This task is about accounting for partnerships.

(a) **Which ONE of the following should be included in a partnership agreement?**

☐ The partnership appropriation account.

☐ Salaries and wages to be paid to all employees.

☐ The rate at which interest is to be allowed on capital.

You have the following information about a partnership business:

Riva, Sam and Terry have been its owners for many years.

On 31 March 20X7, Riva retired from the partnership.
Goodwill was valued at £52,000 and has not yet been entered in the accounting records.

Profit share, effective before the retirement:

Riva 50%
Sam 40%
Terry 10%

Profit share, effective after the retirement:

Sam 70%
Terry 30%

Goodwill is to be introduced into the accounting records on 31 March 20X7 with the partnership change and then immediately eliminated.

(b) **Prepare the goodwill account for the year ended 31 March 20X7, showing clearly the individual entries for the introduction and elimination of goodwill.**

Goodwill account

	£		£
▼		▼	
▼		▼	
▼		▼	
	0		0

Drop-down list:

Balance b/d
Balance c/d
Bank
Capital – Riva
Capital – Sam
Capital – Terry
Current – Riva
Current – Sam
Current – Terry
Drawings
Goodwill

You have the following information about another partnership business:

- The partners are Asma and Ben.
- The financial year ends on 31 December.
- There is no interest on capital or drawings.

Figures relating to the year ended 31 December 20X7 were as follows:

	Asma	Ben
Profit share	60%	40%
Salary entitlement per month	£1,950	£1,400
Sales commission earned during the year	£4,500	£8,300
Drawings	£28,000 over the year	£2,000 each month

Profit for the year ended 31 December 20X7 was £80,000 before appropriations.

(c) **Prepare the appropriation account for the partnership for the year ended 31 December 20X7, and complete the statement below.**

You MUST enter zeros where appropriate in order to obtain full marks.

Use a minus sign for deductions or where there is a loss to be distributed.

Partnership appropriation account for the year ended 31 December 20X7

	£
Profit for appropriation	
▼	
▼	
▼	
▼	
Residual profit available for distribution	
Share of residual profit or loss:	
▼	
▼	
Total residual profit or loss distributed	

Enter any deductions as negative eg -999

Drop-down list:

Drawings – Asma
Drawings – Ben
Salary – Asma
Salary – Ben
Sales commission – Asma
Sales commission – Ben
Share of profit or loss – Asma
Share of profit or loss – Ben

On 3rd January 20X8, Ben takes some goods for personal use.

His current account will be [▼] with their value.

Drop-down list:

debited
credited

Task 6 (21 marks)

This task is about final accounts for partnerships and an introduction to reporting regulations for a limited company.

You are preparing the statement of profit or loss for the Onyx partnership for the year ended 31 March 20X7.

The partners are Jon and Pat, who share profits and losses equally. This is their only entitlement as profit.

You have the final trial balance below. All the necessary year-end adjustments have been made, except for the transfer of profit or loss to the current accounts of the partners.

(a) **Prepare the statement of profit or loss for the Onyx Partnership for the year ended 31 March 20X7.**

If necessary, use a minus sign to indicate ONLY the following:

- **the deduction of an account balance used to make up cost of goods sold**
- **a loss for the year**

Onyx Partnership

Trial balance as at 31 March 20X7

	DR £	CR £
Accruals		1,500
Allowance for doubtful debts		850
Allowance for doubtful debts adjustment		600
Bank	7,888	
Capital – Jon		14,000
Capital – Pat		14,000
Cash	502	
Closing inventory	25,100	25,100
Current – Jon		780
Current – Pat		390
Depreciation charges	9,700	
Furniture at cost	48,500	
Furniture accumulated depreciation		19,400
Loan interest paid	168	
Loan payable		4,000
Office expenses	31,630	
Opening inventory	24,500	
Payroll expenses	16,950	

	DR £	CR £
Prepayments	1,090	
Purchases	153,670	
Purchases ledger control account		21,775
Sales		255,480
Sales ledger control account	30,660	
Selling expenses	10,542	
VAT		3,025
TOTAL	**360,900**	**360,900**

Onyx Partnership

Statement of profit or loss for the year ended 31 March 20X7

	£	£
Sales revenue		
▼		
▼		
▼		
▼		
Cost of goods sold		
Gross profit		
Add:		
▼		
Less:		
▼		
▼		
▼		
▼		
▼		
▼		
Total expenses		
Profit/loss for the year		

Drop-down list:

Accruals
Accumulated depreciation
Allowance for doubtful debts adjustment
Bank
Capital accounts
Closing inventory
Current accounts
Depreciation charges
Loan interest paid
Loan payable
Office expenses
Opening inventory
Payroll expenses
Prepayments
Purchases
Purchases ledger control account
Sales ledger control account
Selling expenses
VAT

(b) **Calculate Jon's share of the profit or loss for the year and his final current account balance.**

Use a minus sign to indicate ONLY a loss for the year, if necessary.

	£
Jon – share of profit or loss	
Jon – final current account balance	

Where will the current account balance for Jon appear on the statement of financial position for Onyx?

Choose ONE:

☐ Within the 'Financed by' section

☐ As a current liability

☐ His current account will not appear on the statement of financial position

Preparation of the final accounts for a limited company at its year end requires more detailed reporting than for a sole trader or partnership.

(c) **Which of the following statements are TRUE for a limited company?**

1. A taxation charge should be shown in the statement of profit or loss.

2. A full analysis of non-current assets must appear on the face of the statement of financial position.

3. Notes to the financial statements are available to third parties.

☐ 1 and 2

☐ 2 and 3

☐ 1 and 3

☐ All of them

AAT AQ2016 SAMPLE ASSESSMENT
FINAL ACCOUNTS PREPARATION

ANSWERS

Final Accounts Preparation
AAT sample assessment

Task 1 (15 marks)

(a) **Find the missing discounts figure by preparing the purchases ledger control account for the year ended 31 March 20X7.**

Purchases ledger control account

		£			£
Balance c/d	▼	14,656	Balance b/d	▼	13,345
Discounts received	▼	2,900	Purchases daybook	▼	149,348
Bank	▼	145,137		▼	
	▼			▼	
		162,693			162,693

(b) **Find the closing balance on the VAT control account for the year ended 31 March 20X7.**

Note: The business is not charged VAT on its rent.

VAT control

		£			£
Purchases daybook	▼	24,408	Balance b/d	▼	1,806
General expenses	▼	1,502	Sales daybook	▼	31,820
Bank	▼	6,169	Cash sales	▼	840
Sales returns daybook	▼	322		▼	
Balance c/d	▼	2,065		▼	
	▼			▼	
		34,466			34,466

(c) **Assuming there are no year-end adjustments, what will be the opening bank account balance in the general ledger as at 1 April 20X7?**

£ | 1,459 | credit | ▼ |

....

Task 2 (15 marks)

(a) **Show whether the following is TRUE or FALSE.**

Gross sales margin percentage may be calculated as: $\dfrac{\text{Gross profit}}{\text{Sales}} \times 100\%$

[✓] True

[ ] False

(b) **Using this information, complete the following tasks.**

(i) **Calculate the cost of goods sold for the year ended 31 March 20X7.**

£ | 48,675 |

(ii) **Calculate the value of closing inventory.**

£ | 4,765 |

You compare this figure with the results of a physical inventory count as at the year end. The total physical inventory value is £350 lower than your calculation above.

(iii) **Which ONE of the following could explain this?**

[ ] Some equipment used in the office was stolen during the year.

[ ] There were unpaid sales invoices at the year end.

[ ] A high value item was included twice in the count.

[✓] The trader has made drawings of goods during the year.

(iv) **Update the value of closing inventory to account for the difference above.**

£ | 4,415 |

The trader has a policy of allowing customers to settle their accounts one month after the sale is made.

(c) **Which of the following is most likely to be the total on the sales ledger at the end of the financial year?**

[✓] £6,940

[ ] £16,225

[ ] £64,900

You are now working on the final accounts of another client.

Your manager is called away unexpectedly. He asks you to undertake a particular task with a deadline during his absence. You know you have not received sufficient training to do this work.

(d) **What should you do? Choose ONE.**

☐ Do the job to the best of your ability and submit the work to the client on time.

☑ Ask if you may have support from elsewhere in the organisation.

☐ Ask a family member who is a qualified accountant to do the work for you.

☐ Advise the client that the deadline will be missed.

Task 3 (18 marks)

(a) **Complete the capital account as of 1 January 20X7, showing clearly the balance carried down.**

Capital

		£			£
Balance c/d	▼	13,000	Bank	▼	13,000
	▼			▼	
	▼			▼	
		13,000			13,000

(b) **Using this information, complete the following tasks:**

(i) **Calculate the value of trade receivables that will appear in the statement of financial position.**

£ 24,460

(ii) **Prepare the statement of financial position for Onyx Trading as at 31 March 20X7.**

Do NOT use brackets, minus signs or dashes.

Onyx Trading

Statement of financial position as at 31 March 20X7

		Cost £	Accumulated depreciation £	Carrying amount £
Non-current assets				
Equipment	▼	32,800	14,350	18,450
Current assets				
Inventory	▼		22,420	
Trade receivables	▼		24,460	
Prepayments	▼		900	
Bank	▼		1,645	
	▼		———	
			49,425	
Current liabilities				
Trade payables	▼	16,720		
Accruals	▼	1,940		
Payroll liabilities	▼	630		
VAT	▼	3,890		
	▼			
			23,180	
Net current assets				26,245
Net assets				44,695

	Cost £	Accumulated depreciation £	Carrying amount £
Financed by:			
Capital			
Opening capital			22,200
Add: Profit for the year ▼			42,495
Less: Drawings ▼			20,000
Closing capital			44,695

(c) **Complete the following:**

Drawings for the year will be transferred as a | debit ▼ | to the capital account in the general ledger.

The opening balance in the capital account on 1 April 20X7 will be: £ | 44,695 |

··

Task 4 (16 marks)

(a) **Complete the following statements:**

(i) **Which ONE of the list below is a benefit of running a business as a sole trader?**

☐ Unlimited liability.

☐ Limited liability.

☑ Complete control over business decisions.

☐ No requirement to prepare annual accounts by a certain date.

(ii) **Complete the sentence:**

A private limited company is owned by its | shareholders. ▼ |

(iii) **Which of the following businesses have owners with limited liability for its debts?**

1. The Joe and Josephine Bloggs Partnership
2. Joe and Josephine Bloggs LLP
3. Joe Bloggs plc

☐ All of them

☐ 3 only

☑ 2 and 3

☐ 1 and 2

(iv) **Complete the following:**

To be a charity, an organisation must satisfy the definition of a charity found in the Charities Act. ▼

Its purpose must be for the benefit of the public. ▼

(b) **Which ONE of the items below prescribes the format of final accounts for an organisation adopting IFRS?**

✓	IAS 1
	IAS 2
	IAS 2012

(c) **Link the boxes to match the following users of final accounts with the most likely reason for their interest. Make each selection by clicking on a box in the left column and then on one in the right column. You can remove a line by clicking on it.**

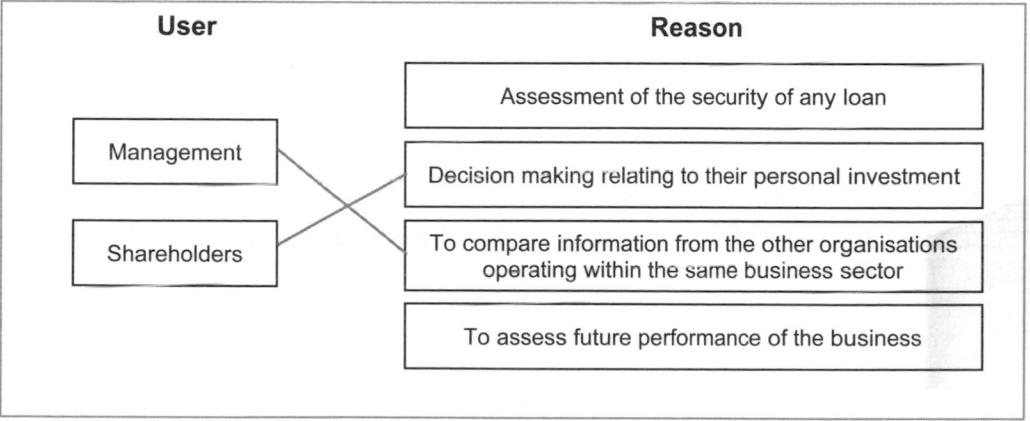

User	Reason
	Assessment of the security of any loan
Management	Decision making relating to their personal investment
Shareholders	To compare information from the other organisations operating within the same business sector
	To assess future performance of the business

Task 5 (15 marks)

(a) **Which ONE of the following should be included in a partnership agreement?**

	The partnership appropriation account.
	Salaries and wages to be paid to all employees.
✓	The rate at which interest is to be allowed on capital.

(b) **Prepare the goodwill account for the year ended 31 March 20X7, showing clearly the individual entries for the introduction and elimination of goodwill.**

Goodwill account

	£			£
Capital – Riva ▼	26,000	Capital – Sam ▼		36,400
Capital – Sam ▼	20,800	Capital – Terry ▼		15,600
Capital – Terry ▼	5,200	▼		
	52,000			52,000

(c) **Prepare the appropriation account for the partnership for the year ended 31 December 20X7, and complete the statement below.**

You MUST enter zeros where appropriate in order to obtain full marks.

Use a minus sign for deductions or where there is a loss to be distributed.

Partnership appropriation account for the year ended 31 December 20X7

	£	
Profit for appropriation	80,000	
Salary – Asma ▼	-23,400	Enter any deductions as negative eg -999
Salary – Ben ▼	-16,800	
Sales commission – Asma ▼	-4,500	
Sales commission – Ben ▼	-8,300	
Residual profit available for distribution	27,000	
Share of residual profit or loss:		
Share of profit or loss – Asma ▼	16,200	
Share of profit or loss – Ben ▼	10,800	
Total residual profit or loss distributed	27,000	

On 3rd January 20X8, Ben takes some goods for personal use.

His current account will be ⎡debited ▼⎤ with their value.

Task 6 (21 marks)

(a) **Prepare the statement of profit or loss for the Onyx Partnership for the year ended 31 March 20X7.**

If necessary, use a minus sign to indicate ONLY the following:

- **the deduction of an account balance used to make up cost of goods sold**
- **a loss for the year**

Onyx Partnership

Statement of profit or loss for the year ended 31 March 20X7

		£	£
Sales revenue			255,480
Opening inventory	▼	24,500	
Purchases	▼	153,670	
Closing inventory	▼	-25,100	
	▼		
Cost of goods sold			153,070
Gross profit			102,410
Add:			
Allowance for doubtful debts adjustment	▼		600
Less:			
Depreciation charges	▼	9,700	
Office expenses	▼	31,630	
Payroll expenses	▼	16,950	
Selling expenses	▼	10,542	
Loan interest paid	▼	168	
	▼		
Total expenses			68,990
Profit/loss for the year			34,020

(b) **Calculate Jon's share of the profit or loss for the year and his final current account balance.**

Use a minus sign to indicate ONLY a loss for the year, if necessary.

	£
Jon – share of profit or loss	17,010
Jon – final current account balance	17,790

Where will the current account balance for Jon appear on the statement of financial position for Onyx?

Choose ONE:

✓	Within the 'Financed by' section
	As a current liability
	His current account will not appear on the statement of financial position

Preparation of the final accounts for a limited company at its year end requires more detailed reporting than for a sole trader or partnership.

(c) **Which of the following statements are TRUE for a limited company?**

1. A taxation charge should be shown in the statement of profit or loss.
2. A full analysis of non-current assets must appear on the face of the statement of financial position.
3. Notes to the financial statements are available to third parties.

	1 and 2
	2 and 3
✓	1 and 3
	All of them

BPP PRACTICE ASSESSMENT 1
FINAL ACCOUNTS PREPARATION

Time allowed: 2 hours

BPP PRACTICE ASSESSMENT 1

Final Accounts Preparation
BPP Practice assessment 1

Task 1

This task is about incomplete records and reconstructing general ledger accounts.

You are working on the financial statements of a business for the year ended 31 March 20X1. You have the following information:

Day book summaries	Goods	VAT	Total
	£	£	£
Sales	125,400	25,080	150,480
Purchases	76,000	15,200	91,200

Balances as at	31 March X0	31 March X1
	£	£
Trade receivables	16,360	15,270
Trade payables	13,280	12,950
Cash in till	300	250

You also find receipts in the cash till for cash purchases of £400.

Bank summary	Dr £		Cr £
Cash banked from till	2,900	Balance b/d	850
Trade receivables	142,650	Administration expenses	3,280
Interest received	520	Trade payables	92,330
		HMRC for VAT	6,820
		Drawings	2,900
		Payroll expenses	12,550
		Balance c/d	27,340
	146,070		146,070

(a) **Using the figures given above, prepare the sales ledger control account for the year ended 31 March 20X1. Show clearly discounts allowed as the balancing figure.**

Sales ledger control account

	£		£

Picklist:

Balance b/d
Balance c/d
Bank
Capital
Cash purchases
Cash sales
Discounts allowed
Discounts received
Drawings
General expenses
Inventory
Purchases day-book
Purchases returns day-book
Sales day-book
Sales returns day-book
Wages

(b) **Find the figure for cash sales by preparing the cash in till account for the year ended 31 March 20X1.**

Note: The business does not charge VAT on its cash sales.

Cash in till

	£		£

You are given the following information about a different sole trader as at 1 November 20XX:

The value of assets and liabilities were:

• Non-current assets at net book value	£17,250
• Trade receivables	£6,250
• Cash at bank	£1,280
• Capital	£21,000

There were no other assets or liabilities, other than trade payables.

(c) **Calculate the trade payables account balance as at 1 November 20XX.**

£ [   ]

(d) **On 30 April 20X0, cash is paid to a credit supplier, with some discount taken. Tick the boxes to show what effect this transaction will have on the balances. You must choose ONE answer for EACH line.**

Balances	Debit ✓	Credit ✓	No change ✓
Income			
Trade receivables			
Trade payables			
Bank			
Expenses			

(e) **Which TWO of the following are accurate representations of the accounting equation? Choose TWO answers.**

	✓
Assets + Liabilities = Capital	
Assets – Liabilities = Capital	
Assets = Liabilities – Capital	
Assets = Liabilities + Capital	

Task 2

This task is about calculating missing balances and the preparation of financial statements.

You have the following information about a sole trader on 1 January 20X4.

- The sole trader started a business and transferred £8,000 of her own money into the business bank account.

- £2,000 was paid from the sole trader's personal credit card for a computer.

- Goods for resale by the business costing £1,500 were purchased from the business bank account.

(a) **Complete the capital account as at 1 January 20X4, showing clearly the balance carried down.**

Capital

	£		£
▼		Balance b/d	
▼		▼	
▼		▼	
▼		▼	
	0		0

Picklist:

Balance b/d
Balance c/d
Bank
Drawings
Computers at cost
Purchases
Purchases ledger control account
Sales
Sales ledger control account
Suspense

At the end of the financial year on 31 December 20X4, you have the following further information:

- Total sales were £45,000.
- Total purchases were £40,000.
- A mark-up of 25% on cost was used throughout the year.

(b) **Calculate the value of the cost of goods sold for the year ended 31 December 20X4.**

£ [ ]

(c) **Calculate the value of inventory as at 31 December 20X4.**

£ [ ]

The trader rented a premises on a busy high street. Her income came only from selling goods in this store.

(d) **Taking into account the information you have, which of the following is most likely to be true?**

Loss for the year was £9,000 ☐

Profit for the year was £9,000 ☐

The trader took drawings from the business during the year.

Now complete the following:

This [▼] explain the profit figure above.

Picklist:

can
cannot

(e) **Which body sets global ethical standards for accountants?**

[ ]

Task 3

This task is about preparing financial statements for sole traders.

You have the following trial balance for a sole trader, Martha Tidfill. All the necessary year-end adjustments have been made.

(a) **Prepare a statement of profit or loss for the business for the year ended 31 August 20X4.**

Martha Tidfill
Trial balance as at 31 August 20X4

	Dr £	Cr £
Accruals		1,250
Bank	2,190	
Capital		20,000
Closing inventory	15,200	15,200
Depreciation expense	4,750	
Discounts allowed	1,920	
Drawings	15,000	
Heat and light	11,620	
Motor vehicles accumulated depreciation		7,600
Motor vehicles at cost	25,400	
Office costs	27,690	
Opening inventory	17,690	
Prepayments	1,120	
Purchases	105,280	
Purchases ledger control account		18,280
Sales		199,560
Sales ledger control account	17,960	
VAT		3,920
Wages	19,990	
	265,810	265,810

Martha Tidfill
Statement of profit or loss for the year ended 31 August 20X4

	£	£
Sales revenue		
Cost of goods sold		
Gross profit		
Total expenses		
Profit/(loss) for the year		

(b) **Indicate where the accruals balance should be shown in the financial statements. Choose ONE from:**

	✓
Non-current assets	
Current assets	
Current liabilities	
Non-current liabilities	

Task 4

This task is about the knowledge and understanding underpinning final accounts preparation.

(a) (i) **Which of the following statements is TRUE?**

1. Limited company status means that a company is only allowed to trade up to a predetermined turnover level in any one year.

2. For organisations that have limited company status, ownership and control are legally separate.

3. The benefit of being a sole trader is that you have no personal liability for the debts of your business.

4. Ordinary partnerships offer the same benefits as limited companies but are usually formed by professionals such as doctors and solicitors.

☐ 1

☐ 2

☐ 3

☐ 4

(ii) **The following are either characteristics of a co-operative or of a public limited company.**

1. Maximising the excess of income over expenditure not a primary objective.

2. Members can vote according to the number of shares owned.

3. Shares can be bought and sold through personal transactions of the members.

4. All members are invited to attend the annual general meeting and participate in decisions at the meeting.

Which of the above are the characteristics of public limited companies?

☐ 2, 3 and 4

☐ 2 and 3 only

☐ 1 and 4 only

☐ 3 and 4 only

(iii) In a limited company, or plc, it is the ultimate responsibility of the [_____ ▼] to take reasonable steps to prevent and detect fraud.

Picklist:

Audit committee

Board of directors

External auditor

(iv) **Which of the following statements about accounting information is incorrect?**

1. Some companies voluntarily provide specially-prepared financial information to employees.

2. Accounting information should be relevant, reliable, complete, objective and timely.

3. Accountants have a strong obligation to ensure that company accounts conform to accounting standards.

4. Charities and professional bodies do not have to produce financial statements in the same way as businesses.

☐ 1

☐ 2

☐ 3

☐ 4

(b) **The two fundamental qualitative characteristics of financial information, according to the IASB's *Conceptual Framework* are:**

☐☐☐☐☐☐☐☐☐☐ **and** ☐☐☐☐☐☐☐☐☐☐

(c) **Which of the following groups are the owners of a limited company?**

1. Non-executive directors.

2. Stakeholders.

3. Shareholders.

☐ 1

☐ 2

☐ 3

Task 5

This task is about partnership accounts.

You have the following information about a partnership business:

- The financial year ends on 31 July.

- The partners at the beginning of the year were Grace and Harry.

- Jamal was admitted to the partnership on 1 February 20X6.

- Partners' annual salaries, effective to 31 January 20X6:

    - Grace   £15,600
    - Harry   £19,200
    - Jamal   Nil

- Partners' annual salaries, effective from 1 February 20X6:

    - Grace   £13,200
    - Harry   £16,800
    - Jamal   £6,000

- Partners' interest on capital:

    - Grace   £800 per full year
    - Harry   £1,000 per full year
    - Jamal   £500 per full year

- Profit share, effective until 31 January 20X6:

    - Grace   30%
    - Harry   70%

- Profit share, effective from 1 February 20X6:

    - Grace   40%
    - Harry   50%
    - Jamal   10%

Profit for the year ended 31 July 20X6 was £120,000. You can assume that profits accrued evenly during the year.

Prepare the appropriation account for the partnership for the year ended 31 July 20X6.

Partnership appropriation account for the year ended 31 July 20X6

	1 August X5 – 31 January X6 £	1 February X6 – 31 July X6 £	Total £
Profit for the year			
Salaries:			
Grace			
Harry			
Jamal			
Interest on capital:			
Grace			
Harry			
Jamal			
Profit available for distribution			
Profit share			
Grace			
Harry			
Jamal			
Total profit distributed			

Task 6

Partnership statement of financial position

This task is about preparing a partnership statement of financial position.

You are preparing the statement of financial position for the Jessop Partnership for the year ended 31 October 20X7. The partners are Malcolm and Rose.

All the necessary year end adjustments have been made, except for the transfer of profit to the current accounts of the partners.

Before sharing profits the balances of the partners' current accounts are:

- Malcolm   £400 debit
- Rose   £230 credit

Each partner is entitled to £7,250 profit share.

(a) **Calculate the credit balance of each partner's current account after sharing profits. Fill in the answers below.**

Current account balance: Malcolm	£
Current account balance: Rose	£

Note: these balances will need to be transferred into the statement of financial position of the partnership which follows.

You have the following trial balance. All the necessary year-end adjustments have been made.

(b) **Prepare a statement of financial position for the partnership as at 31 October 20X7. You need to use the partners' current account balances that you have just calculated. Do NOT use brackets, minus signs or dashes.**

Jessop Partnership
Trial balance as at 31 October 20X7

	Dr £	Cr £
Accruals		970
Allowance for doubtful debts		1,280
Allowance for doubtful debts adjustment	130	
Bank		2,140
Capital – Malcolm		18,000
Capital – Rose		22,000
Cash	250	
Closing inventory	9,450	9,450
Current account – Malcolm	400	
Current account – Rose		230
Depreciation expense	2,440	
Disposal of non-current asset	2,100	
Furniture & fittings accumulated depreciation		9,240
Furniture & fittings at cost	32,980	
Marketing	17,930	
Opening inventory	21,780	
Purchases	88,810	
Purchases ledger control account		7,620
Sales		179,610
Sales ledger control account	35,090	
Wages	41,370	
VAT		2,190
Total	252,730	252,730

Jessop Partnership
Statement of financial position as at 31 October 20X7

	Cost £	Depreciation £	Carrying amount £
Non-current assets			
Current assets			
Current liabilities			
Net current assets			
Net assets			
Financed by:	Malcolm	Rose	Total

(c) IAS 1 *Presentation of Financial Statements* requires some items to be presented as separate line items in the financial statements and others to be disclosed in the notes.

1   Depreciation
2   Revenue
3   Closing inventories
4   Finance cost
5   Dividends

Which two of the above have to be shown as line items in the statement of profit or loss and other comprehensive income, rather than in the notes to the financial statements?

1 and 4	
3 and 5	
2 and 3	
2 and 4	

BPP PRACTICE ASSESSMENT 1
FINAL ACCOUNTS PREPARATION

ANSWERS

Final Accounts Preparation
BPP practice assessment 1

Task 1

(a) **Sales ledger control account**

	£		£
Balance b/d	16,360	Bank	142,650
Sales day book	150,480	Discounts allowed	8,920
		Balance c/d	15,270
	166,840		166,840

(b) **Cash in till**

	£		£
Balance b/d	300	Cash purchases	400
Cash sales	3,250	Cash banked	2,900
		Balance c/d	250
	3,550		3,550

(c)

£	3,780

(17,250 + 6,250 + 1,280 – 21,000)

(d)

Balances	Debit ✓	Credit ✓	No change ✓
Income		✓	
Trade receivables			✓
Trade payables	✓		
Bank		✓	
Expenses			✓

(e)

	✓
Assets + Liabilities = Capital	
Assets – Liabilities = Capital	✓
Assets = Liabilities - Capital	
Assets = Liabilities + Capital	✓

Task 2

(a) **Capital**

	£		£
		Balance b/d	0
		Bank	8,000
Balance c/d	10,000	Computers	2,000
	10,000		10,000

(b) **£** | 36,000 | **Working:** £45,000 ×100/125

(c) **£** | 4,000 | **Working:** £40,000 - £36,000

(d) Loss for the year was £9,000   ✓

Profit for the year was £9,000   ☐

This | cannot | explain the profit figure above.

Note: Gross profit is £9,000 (£45,000 – £36,000). The business premises is rented, therefore rent is an expense, which means that the profit for the year is not £9,000.

Drawings are not included as expenses in profit or loss.

(e) International Ethics Standards Board for Accountants (IESBA)

Task 3

(a)

Martha Tidfill
Statement of profit or loss for the year ended 31 August 20X4

	£	£
Sales revenue		199,560
Opening inventory	17,690	
Purchases	105,280	
Closing inventory	(15,200)	
Cost of goods sold		(107,770)
Gross profit		91,790
Less:		
Depreciation expense	4,750	
Discounts allowed	1,920	
Heat and light	11,620	
Office costs	27,690	
Wages	19,990	
Total expenses		(65,970)
Profit for the year		25,820

(b)

	✓
Non-current assets	
Current assets	
Current liabilities	✓
Non-current liabilities	

Task 4

(a) (i) ☐ 1

☑ 2

☐ 3

☐ 4

(ii) ☑ 2, 3 and 4

☐ 2 and 3 only

☐ 1 and 4 only

☐ 3 and 4 only

(iii) In a limited company, or plc, it is the ultimate responsibility of the

| Board of directors |

to take reasonable steps to prevent and detect fraud.

(iv) ☐ 1

☐ 2

☐ 3

☑ 4

(b)

| Relevance | and | Faithful representation |

(c) ☐ 1

☐ 2

☑ 3

Task 5

Partnership appropriation account for the year ended 31 July 20X6

	1 August X5 – 31 January X6 £	1 February X6 – 31 July X6 £	Total £
Profit for the year	60,000	60,000	120,000
Salaries:			
Grace	7,800	6,600	14,400
Harry	9,600	8,400	18,000
Jamal	0	3,000	3,000
Interest on capital:			
Grace	400	400	800
Harry	500	500	1,000
Jamal	0	250	250
Profit available for distribution	41,700	40,850	82,550

Profit share			
Grace	12,510	16,340	28,850
Harry	29,190	20,425	49,615
Jamal	0	4,085	4,085
Total profit distributed	41,700	40,850	82,550

Task 6

(a)

Current account balance: Malcolm	£	6,850	**Working:** £7,250 – £400
Current account balance: Rose	£	7,480	£7,250 + £230

(b) **Jessop Partnership**
Statement of financial position as at 31 October 20X7

	Cost £	Depreciation £	Carrying amount £
Non-current assets	32,980	9,240	23,740
Current assets			
Inventory		9,450	
Receivables (35,090 – 1,280)		33,810	
Cash		250	
		43,510	
Current liabilities			
Accruals	970		
Payables	7,620		
Bank overdraft	2,140		
VAT	2,190		
		12,920	
Net current assets			30,590
Net assets			54,330
Financed by:	Malcolm	Rose	Total
Capital accounts	18,000	22,000	40,000
Current accounts	6,850	7,480	14,330
			54,330

(c)

1 and 4	
3 and 5	
2 and 3	
2 and 4	✓

BPP PRACTICE ASSESSMENT 2
FINAL ACCOUNTS PREPARATION

Time allowed: 2 hours

Final Accounts Preparation
BPP practice assessment 2

Task 1

This task is about incomplete records and reconstructing general ledger accounts.

You are working on the accounting records of a sole trader for the year ended 31 May 20X4. You have the following information:

Day-book summaries:	Goods £	VAT £	Total £
Sales	89,000	17,800	106,800
Sales returns	2,500	500	3,000
Purchases	56,000	11,200	67,200
Purchases returns	None		

Further information:	Net £	VAT £	Total £
General expenses	1,050	210	1,260

Balances as at:	31 May 20X3 £	31 May 20X4 £
Trade receivables	13,000	8,500
Trade payables	9,250	11,250
Closing inventory	3,260	4,650
VAT	555 credit	Not available
Bank	Not available	10,500 debit

- Cash sales of £1,000 were made, excluding VAT at 20%. The total banked was posted to the cash sales account.

- All purchases are on credit terms.

Receipts and payments recorded in the bank account comprise:	£
Amounts from credit customers	98,000
Amounts to credit suppliers	60,300
Amounts banked from cash sales	4,800
Loan receipt	3,000
Rent paid	6,350
General expenses	1,260
HMRC for VAT – payment	1,500
Drawings	12,000
Wages	13,000

(a) **Find the missing discounts figure by preparing the purchases ledger control account for the year ended 31 May 20X4.**

Purchases ledger control account

	£		£
▼		▼	
▼		▼	
▼		▼	
▼		▼	
	0		0

Picklist:

Balance b/d, Balance c/d, Bank, Cash purchases, Cash sales, Discounts allowed, Discounts received, Drawings, General expenses, Inventory, Loan, Purchases day-book, Rent, Sales day-book, Sales returns day-book, Wages, <Empty>

(b) **Find the closing balance on the VAT control account for the year ended 31 May 20X4. Note: The business is not charged VAT on its rent.**

VAT control

	£		£
▼		▼	
▼		▼	
▼		▼	
▼		▼	
▼		▼	
▼		▼	

Picklist:

Balance b/d, Balance c/d, Bank, Capital, Cash sales, Discounts allowed, Discounts received, Drawings, General expenses, Loan, Purchases day-book, Rent, Sales day-book, Sales returns day-book, Wages, <Empty>

The totals recorded in the cashbook for the year ended 31 May 20X4 were:

Receipts	£105,800
Payments	£94,410

(c) **Assuming there are no year-end adjustments, what was the opening balance in the cashbook as at 31 May 20X3?**

£ [   ]   [▼]

Picklist:

Debit, Credit

Task 2

This task is about calculating missing balances and the preparation of financial statements.

(a) On 1 January 20X8, a business had assets of £20,000 and liabilities of £14,000. By 31 December 20X8 it had assets of £30,000 and liabilities of £20,000. The owner had contributed capital of £8,000 during the year.

Use the T account below to calculate how much profit or loss the business had made over the year.

£ [   ]

Capital account

	£		£

You are given the following information about a different business, a shop, for one financial year:

Sales were £95,200 in the year, all at a mark-up of 60%. The opening inventory was £22,560 and the closing inventory was £18,420.

(b) **Calculate the cost of goods sold figure for the year.**

£ [   ]

(c) **Calculate the purchases figure for the year.**

£ [   ]

(d) **Identify whether each of the following balances is presented as a current asset, a current liability or neither on the face of the statement of financial position.**

Balances	Current asset ✓	Current liability ✓	Neither ✓
Accrual			
Opening inventory			
Prepayment			
Loan from bank payable in five years			
Bank overdraft			

(e) Professional accountants must maintain the confidentiality of information which is obtained in circumstances that give rise to a duty of confidentiality.

Is this an ethical principle only, a legal obligation only, or both an ethical principle and a legal obligation?

▼

Picklist:

Ethical principle only
Legal obligation only
Both an ethical principle and a legal obligation

Task 3

This task is about preparing financial statements for sole traders.

You have the following trial balance for a sole trader, Tom Kassam. All the necessary year-end adjustments have been made.

(a) **Prepare a statement of profit or loss for the business for the year ended 31 May 20X6.**

Tom Kassam
Trial balance as at 31 May 20X6

	Dr £	Cr £
Accruals		980
Administration expenses	12,060	
Bank	1,730	
Capital		14,000
Closing inventory	14,320	
Depreciation expense	3,880	
Discounts allowed	1,470	
Distribution expenses	25,340	
Drawings	17,790	
Furniture & fittings accumulated depreciation		6,480
Furniture & fittings at cost	24,800	
Prepayments	1,260	
Cost of goods sold	98,500	
Purchases ledger control account		15,940
Sales		201,560
Sales ledger control account	18,450	
VAT		2,970
Wages	22,330	
	241,930	241,930

Tom Kassam
Statement of profit or loss for the year ended 31 May 20X6

	£	£
Sales revenue		
Cost of goods sold		
Gross profit		
Total expenses		
Profit/(loss) for the year		

(b) **Indicate where the VAT balance should be shown in the financial statements. Choose ONE from:**

	✓
Non-current assets	
Current assets	
Current liabilities	
Non-current liabilities	

(c) **Which of the following amounts will appear in both the statement of profit or loss and the statement of financial position?**

	✓
Drawings	
Capital	
Opening inventory	
Closing inventory	

Task 4

This task is about the knowledge and understanding underpinning final accounts preparation.

(a) (i) **Which of the following is a benefit of running a business as a sole trader?**

1. No formal procedures to set up the business.

2. The business is highly dependent on the owner.

3. An absence of economies of scale.

☐ 1

☐ 2

☐ 3

(ii) **Which of the following statements regarding Limited Liability Partnerships is correct?**

1. A written partnership agreement is required to form the partnership.

2. The partnership dissolves when a partner leaves.

3. The partnership must have two designated members who are responsible for the publicity requirements of the partnership.

4. The partnership is exempt from audit.

☐ 1

☐ 2

☐ 3

☐ 4

(iii) Which type of company does not have share capital?

1. An unlimited liability company

2. A public company

3. A company limited by guarantee

☐ 1

☐ 2

☐ 3

(iv) **ADB is a business which is owned by its workers. The workers share the profits and they each have a vote on how the business is run.**

Which of the following best describes ADB?

1. Public sector.

2. Private sector.

3. Not-for-profit.

4. Co-operative

☐ 1

☐ 2

☐ 3

☐ 4

(b) **According to IAS 1 Presentation of Financial Statements which of the following does not represent an objective of financial statements?**

1. To provide information to investors in making economic decisions.

2. To provide information to managers in making business decisions.

3. To show the results of management's stewardship of the resources entrusted to it.

4. To help users predict the entity's future cash flows

☐ 1

☐ 2

☐ 3

☐ 4

(c) **Which of the following statements regarding ordinary share capital is correct?**

1. Dividends must be paid on ordinary share capital every financial year.

2. On liquidation of the company, ordinary shares entitle the shareholder to have their capital repaid ahead of other creditors.

3. Ordinary shares may or may not have voting rights attached.

☐ 1

☐ 2

☐ 3

Task 5

This task is about accounting for partnerships.

You have the following information about a partnership:

The partners are Nigel and Paula.

- Gavin was admitted to the partnership on 1 June 20X7 when he paid £18,500 into the bank account.

- Profit share, effective until 31 May 20X7:

  - Nigel   25%
  - Paula   75%

- Profit share, effective from 1 June 20X7:

  - Nigel   30%
  - Paula   50%
  - Gavin   20%

- Goodwill was valued at £50,000 on 31 May 20X7.

- Goodwill is to be introduced into the partners' capital accounts on 31 May and then eliminated on 1 June.

(a) **Prepare the capital account for Gavin, the new partner, showing clearly the balance carried down as at 1 June 20X7.**

Capital account – Gavin

	£		£

(b) **Identify whether each of the following statements is true or false.**

	True ✓	False ✓
When a partner retires from a partnership, they must always be paid what they are owed in cash.		
If the partners agree to change their profit shares, this must take effect from the beginning of the accounting period whatever the partners may agree between themselves.		

Task 6

This task is about partnership accounts.

You have the following information about a partnership:

- The financial year ends on 30 September 20X5.

- The partners are William, Richard and Steve.

- Partners' annual salaries:

    - William £15,600
    - Richard £17,200
    - Steve   £12,900

- Partners' capital account balances as at 30 September 20X5:

    - William £100,000
    - Richard £80,000
    - Steve   £60,000

Interest on capital is charged at 1% per annum on the capital account balance at the end of the financial year.

- The partners share the remaining profit of £72,000 as follows:

    - William 30%
    - Richard 45%
    - Steve   25%

- Partners' drawings for the year:

    - William £22,890
    - Richard £51,250
    - Steve   £17,240

Prepare the current accounts for the partners for the year ended 30 September 20X5. Show clearly the balances carried down. You MUST enter zeros where appropriate in order to obtain full marks. Do NOT use brackets, minus signs or dashes.

Current accounts

	William £	Richard £	Steve £		William £	Richard £	Steve £
Balance b/d	0	1,230	950	Balance b/d	200	0	0

Which of the following is the best description of fair presentation in accordance with IAS 1 *Presentation of Financial Statements*?

1. The financial statements are accurate

2. The financial statements are as accurate as possible given the accounting systems of the organisation

3. The directors of the company have stated that the financial statements are accurate and correctly prepared

4. The financial statements are reliable in that they reflect the effects of transactions, other events and conditions

☐ 1

☐ 2

☐ 3

☐ 4

BPP PRACTICE ASSESSMENT 2
FINAL ACCOUNTS PREPARATION

ANSWERS

Final Accounts Preparation
BPP practice assessment 2

Task 1

(a) **Purchases ledger control account**

		£			£
Bank	▼	60,300	Balance b/d	▼	9,250
Discounts received	▼	4,900	Purchase day-book	▼	67,200
Balance c/d	▼	11,250		▼	
	▼	___		▼	___
		76,450			76,450

(b) **VAT control**

		£			£
Purchase day-book	▼	11,200	Balance b/d	▼	555
General expenses	▼	210	Sales day-book	▼	17,800
Bank	▼	1,500	Cash sales	▼	200
Sales returns day-book	▼	500		▼	
Balance c/d	▼	5,145		▼	
	▼	___		▼	___
		18,555			18,555

(c) £ | 890 | | credit | ▼ | **Working:** £10,500 + £94,410 - £105,800

Task 2

(a)

£	4,000 loss

Workings:

	£
Assets 1 January 20X8	20,000
Liabilities 1 January 20X8	14,000
Owner's capital at 1 January 20X8	6,000

	£
Assets 31 December 20X8	30,000
Liabilities 31 December 20X8	20,000
Owner's capital at 31 December 20X8	10,000

Capital account

	£		£
Loss (bal fig)	4,000	Balance b/d	6,000
Balance c/d	10,000	Capital introduced	8,000
	14,000		14,000

(b)

£	59,500

(c)

£	55,360

Workings:

	£	%
Sales revenue	95,200	160
Cost of goods sold (95,200 x 100/160)	59,500	100
Gross profit	35,700	60
Opening inventory	22,560	
Purchases (bal fig)	55,360	
Closing inventory	(18,420)	
Cost of goods sold (from above)	59,500	

(d)

Balances	Current asset ✓	Current liability ✓	Neither ✓
Accrual		✓	
Opening inventory			✓
Prepayment	✓		
Loan from bank payable in five years			✓
Bank overdraft		✓	

(e) BOTH an ethical principle and a legal obligation

Task 3

(a)

Tom Kassam
Statement of profit or loss for the year ended 31 May 20X6

	£	£
Sales revenue		201,560
Cost of goods sold		(98,500)
Gross profit		103,060
Less:		
Depreciation expense	3,880	
Discounts allowed	1,470	
Distribution expenses	25,340	
Administration expenses	12,060	
Wages	22,330	
Total expenses		(65,080)
Profit for the year		37,980

(b)

	✓
Non-current assets	
Current assets	
Current liabilities	✓
Non-current liabilities	

(c)

	✓
Drawings	
Capital	
Opening inventory	
Closing inventory	✓

....

Task 4

(a) (i)   ☑ 1

         ☐ 2

         ☐ 3

  (ii)   ☐ 1

         ☐ 2

         ☑ 3

         ☐ 4

  (iii)   ☐ 1

         ☐ 2

         ☑ 3

Companies limited by guarantee do not have share capital.

  (iv)   ☐ 1

         ☐ 2

         ☐ 3

         ☑ 4

(b) ☐ 1

　　☑ 2

　　☐ 3

　　☐ 4

(c) ☐ 1

　　☐ 2

　　☑ 3

Task 5

(a) **Capital account – Gavin**

	£		£
Goodwill	10,000	Balance b/d	0
Balance c/d	8,500	Bank	18,500
	18,500		18,500

(b)

	True ✓	False ✓
When a partner retires from a partnership, they must always be paid what they are owed in cash.		✓
If the partners agree to change their profit shares, this must take effect from the beginning of the accounting period whatever the partners may agree between themselves.		✓

Task 6

Current accounts

	William £	Richard £	Steve £		William £	Richard £	Steve £
Balance b/d	0	1,230	950	Balance b/d	200	0	0
Drawings	22,890	51,250	17,240	Salaries	15,600	17,200	12,900
Balance c/d	15,510	0	13,310	Interest on capital	1,000	800	600
				Profit share	21,600	32,400	18,000
				Balance c/d	0	2,080	0
	38,400	52,480	31,500		38,400	52,480	31,500

☐ 1

☐ 2

☐ 3

☑ 4

BPP PRACTICE ASSESSMENT 3
FINAL ACCOUNTS PREPARATION

Time allowed: 2 hours

BPP PRACTICE
ASSESSMENT 3

BPP
LEARNING MEDIA

Final Accounts Preparation
BPP practice assessment 3

Task 1

This task is about incomplete records and reconstructing general ledger accounts.

You are working on the financial statements of a business for the year ended 31 March 20X1. The business is not registered for VAT. You have the following information:

	Balance at 31 March 20X0	Balance at 31 March 20X1
Trade receivables	39,000	27,500
Trade payables	15,600	18,950

Discounts allowed during the year amounted to £7,400 and discounts received were £2,610. A contra entry of £830 was made between the sales and purchases ledger control accounts.

Bank account summary

	£		£
Balance b/d	59,150	Sundry expenses	460
Trade receivables	195,240	Trade payables	84,230
Rental income	1,500	Wages	34,780
		Drawings	12,000
		Balance c/d	124,420
	255,890		255,890

(a) **Calculate the figure for sales for the year by preparing the sales ledger control account.**

Sales ledger control account

	£		£

(b) **Calculate the figure for purchases for the year by preparing the purchases ledger control account.**

Purchases ledger control account

	£		£

(c) At 1 January 20X5 suppliers were owed £20,000, by 31 December 20X5 they were owed £16,000. In the year, receivables and payables contras were £7,000, and £700 of debit balances were transferred to receivables. Credit purchases were £120,000 and £5,000 of discounts were received.

What was paid to suppliers during the year?

	✓
£111,300	
£112,000	
£112,700	
£116,000	

Task 2

(a) This task is about calculating missing balances and the preparation of financial statements.

A business had net assets at the start of the year of £47,390 and at the end of the year of £57,150. The business made a profit of £34,740 for the year.

Use the T account below to calculate the drawings made by the owner in the year.

£	

Capital account

	£		£
	_____		_____
	=====		=====

You are given the following information about a shop for one financial year:

Sales for the year amounted to £42,000, the opening inventory was £4,700 and purchases were £30,000. Gross profit margin is 33⅓%.

(b) **Calculate the figure for cost of goods sold.**

£ [   ]

(c) **Calculate the figure for closing inventory.**

£ [   ]

(d) **The proprietor takes goods that had cost the business £250 from the shop for her own personal consumption. Tick the boxes to show the effect of this on the accounts of the business. You must choose ONE answer for EACH line.**

	Debit ✓	Credit ✓	No effect ✓
Bank			
Drawings			
Inventory			
Purchases			

(e) Marion, a professional accountant in practice, gives Larch Ltd an opinion on the application of accounting principles to the company's specific transactions. Marion knew that she was forming her opinion on the basis of inadequate information.

In addition to integrity, state which other ONE of Marion's fundamental ethical principles is threatened by this situation.

[   ]

Task 3

This task is about preparing financial statements for sole traders.

You have the following trial balance for a sole trader, Colin Woodward. All the necessary year-end adjustments have been made.

(a) **Prepare a statement of profit or loss for the business for the year ended 31 March 20X0.**

Colin Woodward
Trial balance as at 31 March 20X0

	Dr £	Cr £
Sales revenue		218,396
Cost of goods sold	79,474	
Discounts allowed	3,260	
Trade receivables and payables	22,863	8,367
Non-current assets at cost	57,150	
Accumulated depreciation		24,840
Motor expenses	1,374	
Wages and salaries	84,381	
Bank balance	2,654	
Rent, rates and insurance	28,012	
General expenses	4,111	
Capital		65,373
Heat and light	12,241	
Closing inventory	13,142	
Deprecation charge	8,314	
	316,976	316,976

Colin Woodward
Statement of profit or loss for the year ended 31 March 20X0

	£	£
Sales revenue		
Cost of goods sold		
Gross profit		
Total expenses		
Profit/(loss) for the year		

(b) **Which of the following best explains the term 'current asset'?**

	✓
An asset currently in use by a business	
Something a business has or uses, likely to be held for only a short time	
An amount owed to somebody else which is due for repayment soon	
Money which the business currently has in its bank account	

(c) **Which of the following statements concerning journal entries is correct?**

	✓
Journal entries need not be authorised	
Journal entries are used only to correct errors	
The journal is one of the ledgers of the business	
All journal entries must have a narrative explanation	

Task 4

This task is about the knowledge and understanding underpinning final accounts preparation.

(a) (i) **Which of the following statements regarding sole traders is correct?**

    1.   The business is legally distinct from the owner.

    2.   All of a sole trader's profits accrue to the owner.

    3.   Sole traders do not need to register for VAT.

☐ 1

☐ 2

☐ 3

(ii) **In a company limited by shares, what is the limit of a member's liability?**

    1.   The amount they guaranteed to pay in the event of the company being wound-up.

    2.   The amount of share capital they have purchased, including any amounts outstanding on the shares that they own.

    3.   Nothing, the company is liable for its own debts.

☐ 1

☐ 2

☐ 3

(iii) A group of friends wish to set up a business. They wish to limit their liability for the business' debts to an amount that they agree to when the business is formed

Which of the following businesses is most suitable to the needs of the group?

    1.   An unlimited company

    2.   A company limited by shares

    3.   A partnership

    4.   A corporation sole

☐ 1

☐ 2

☐ 3

☐ 4

(iv) **Which of the following indicates that a business is being run as a sole trader?**

1   The business does not employ any employees

2   It does not file accounts with the Registrar of Companies

3   The business is run by one person who is not legally distinct from the business

4   Share capital of the business is not sold on a recognised stock exchange

☐ 1

☐ 2

☐ 3

☐ 4

(b) **In applying fundamental accounting concepts the preparers of financial information are also using which of the following?**

1.   Legislation

2.   Accounting standards

3.   Judgement

4   Financial reporting standards

☐ 1

☐ 2

☐ 3

☐ 4

(c) **For each of the following statements determine which accounting principle or concept is being invoked:**

(i)   Computer software, although for long-term use in the business, is charged to the statement of profit or loss when purchased as its value is small in comparison to the hardware.

Principle/concept	

(ii)   The non-current assets of the business are valued at their carrying amount rather than the value for which they might be sold.

Principle/concept	

(iii)   The expenses that the business incurs during the year are charged as expenses in the statement of profit or loss even if the amount of the expense has not yet been paid in cash.

Principle/concept	

Task 5

This task is about partnership accounts. Note for students: the two parts of this task use the same names but are independent of each other.

(a) **You have the following information about a partnership business:**

- The financial year ends on 31 March.

- The partners at the beginning of the year were James, Kenzie and Lewis.

- James retired on 30 September 20X0.

- Partners' annual salaries:

    – James   £41,000
    – Kenzie   £50,000
    – Lewis   Nil

- Partners' interest on capital:

    – James   £3,000 per full year
    – Kenzie   £3,000 per full year
    – Lewis   £3,000 per full year

- Profit share, effective until 30 September 20X0:

    – James   60%
    – Kenzie   20%
    – Lewis   20%

- Profit share, effective from 1 October 20X0:

    – Kenzie   75%
    – Lewis   25%

Profit for the year ended 31 March 20X1 was £200,000. You can assume that profits accrued evenly during the year.

Prepare the appropriation account for the partnership for the year ended 31 March 20X1.

Partnership appropriation account for the year ended 31 March 20X1

	1 April X0 – 30 September X0 £	1 October X0 – 31 March X1 £	Total £
Profit for the year			
Salaries:			
James			
Kenzie			
Lewis			
Interest on capital:			
James			
Kenzie			
Lewis			
Profit available for distribution			

Profit share			
James			
Kenzie			
Lewis			
Total profit distributed			

(b) **You have the following different information about the partnership:**

- The financial year ends on 31 March.

- The partners are James, Kenzie and Lewis.

- Partners' annual salaries:

  - James   £16,500
  - Kenzie   £36,000
  - Lewis   nil

- Partners' capital account balances as at 31 March 20X1:

  - James   £50,000
  - Kenzie   £100,000
  - Lewis   £100,000

Interest on capital is charged at 6% per annum on the capital account balance at the end of the financial year.

- The partners share the remaining profit of £80,000 as follows:

  - James   30%
  - Kenzie   50%
  - Lewis   20%

- Partners' drawings for the year:

  - James   £32,000
  - Kenzie   £80,000
  - Lewis   £26,000

Prepare the current accounts for the partners for the year ended 31 March 20X1. Show clearly the balances carried down. You MUST enter zeros where appropriate in order to obtain full marks. Do NOT use brackets, minus signs or dashes.

Current accounts

	James £	Kenzie £	Lewis £		James £	Kenzie £	Lewis £
Balance b/d	800	0	0	Balance b/d	0	3,000	8,600

Task 6

Partnership statement of financial position

This task is about preparing a partnership statement of financial position.

You are preparing the statement of financial position for the Jasper Partnership for the year ended 31 March 20X1. The partners are Aldo and Billy.

All the necessary year-end adjustments have been made, except for the transfer of profit to the current accounts of the partners.

Before sharing profits the balances of the partners' current accounts are:

- Aldo £366 credit
- Billy £600 credit

Each partner is entitled to £7,500 profit share.

(a) **Calculate the balance of each partner's current account after sharing profits. Fill in the answers below.**

Current account balance: Aldo	£	
Current account balance: Billy	£	

Note: these balances will need to be transferred into the statement of financial position of the partnership which follows.

You have the following trial balance. All the necessary year-end adjustments have been made.

(b) **Prepare a statement of financial position for the partnership as at 31 March 20X1. You need to use the partners' current account balances that you have just calculated. Do NOT use brackets, minus signs or dashes.**

Jasper Partnership
Statement of financial position as at 31 March 20X1

	Dr £	Cr £
Accruals		1,190
Administration expenses	39,230	
Bank	4,276	
Capital – Aldo		35,000
Capital – Billy		20,000
Cash	690	
Closing inventory	20,570	20,570
Current account – Aldo		366
Current account – Billy		600
Depreciation charge	4,525	
Disposal of non-current asset	750	
Motor vehicles at cost	43,500	
Motor vehicles accumulated depreciation		12,125
Opening inventory	23,027	
Allowance for doubtful debts		830
Purchases	104,250	
Purchases ledger control account		32,950
Sales		178,785
Sales ledger control account	53,765	
Selling expenses	12,573	
VAT		4,740
Total	307,156	307,156

Jasper Partnership
Trial balance as at 31 March 20X1

	Cost £	Depreciation £	Carrying amount £
Non-current assets			
Current assets			
Current liabilities			
Net current assets			
Net assets			
Financed by:	Aldo	Billy	Total

(c) According to IAS 1 *Presentation of Financial Statements*, compliance with International Accounting Standards and International Financial Reporting Standards will normally ensure that:

1. The entity's inventory is valued at net realisable value

2. The entity's assets are valued at their break-up value

3. The entity's financial statements are prepared on the assumption that it is a going concern

4. The entity's financial position, financial performance and cash flows are presented fairly

☐ 1

☐ 2

☐ 3

☐ 4

BPP PRACTICE ASSESSMENT 3
FINAL ACCOUNTS PREPARATION

ANSWERS

Final Accounts Preparation
BPP practice assessment 3

Task 1

(a) **Sales ledger control account**

	£		£
Balance b/d	39,000	Bank	195,240
Sales (bal. fig)	191,970	Discounts allowed	7,400
		Contra with PLCA	830
		Balance c/d	27,500
	230,970		230,970

(b) **Purchases ledger control account**

	£		£
Bank	84,230	Balance b/d	15,600
Discounts received	2,610	Purchases (bal. fig)	91,020
Contra with SLCA	830		
Balance c/d	18,950		
	106,620		106,620

(c)

	✓
£111,300	
£112,000	
£112,700	✓
£116,000	

Workings:

Payables control account

	£		£
Contra	7,000	Balance b/d	20,000
Discounts received	5,000	Transfers to receivables	700
Cash paid (bal fig)	112,700	Purchases	120,000
Balance c/d	16,000		
	140,700		140,700

Task 2

(a)

£	24,980

Workings:

Capital account

	£		£
Drawings (bal fig)	24,980	Balance b/d	47,390
Balance c/d	57,150	Profit	34,740
	82,130		82,130

(b)

£	28,000

(c)

£	6,700

Workings:

	£	%
Sales revenue	42,000	100
Cost of goods sold	28,000	66⅔
Gross profit	14,000	33⅓
Opening inventory	4,700	
Purchases	30,000	
Closing inventory (balancing figure)	(6,700)	
Cost of goods sold (from above)	28,000	

(d)

	Debit ✓	Credit ✓	No effect ✓
Bank			✓
Drawings	✓		
Inventory			✓
Purchases		✓	

(e) Professional competence and due care. Marion is not acting diligently nor is she in accordance with applicable professional standards by giving an opinion without having access to adequate information. Professional competence and due care. Marion is not acting diligently nor is she in accordance with applicable professional standards by giving an opinion without having access to adequate information.

Task 3

(a) **Colin Woodward**
Statement of profit or loss for the year ended 31 March 20X0

	£	£
Sales revenue		218,396
Cost of goods sold		(79,474)
Gross profit		138,922
Less:		
Discounts allowed	3,260	
Motor expenses	1,374	
Heat and light	12,241	
Rent, rates and insurance	28,012	
Wages and salaries	84,381	
General expenses	4,111	
Depreciation	8,314	
Total expenses		(141,693)
Profit/(loss) for the year		(2,771)

(b)

	✓
An asset currently in use by a business	
Something a business has or uses, likely to be held for only a short time	✓
An amount owed to somebody else which is due for repayment soon	
Money which the business currently has in its bank account	

(c)

	✓
Journal entries need not be authorised	
Journal entries are used only to correct errors	
The journal is one of the ledgers of the business	
All journal entries must have a narrative explanation	✓

Task 4

(a) (i)
- ☐ 1
- ☑ 2
- ☐ 3

(ii)
- ☐ 1
- ☑ 2
- ☐ 3

(iii)
- ☐ 1
- ☑ 2
- ☐ 3
- ☐ 4

(iv)
- ☐ 1
- ☐ 2
- ☑ 3
- ☐ 4

(b)
- ☐ 1
- ☐ 2
- ☑ 3
- ☐ 4

(c) (i)

Principle/concept	Materiality

(ii)

Principle/concept	Going concern

(iii)

Principle/concept	Accruals or matching

Task 5

(a) Partnership appropriation account for the year ended 31 March 20X1

	1 April X0 – 30 September X0 £	1 October X0 – 31 March X1 £	Total £
Profit for the year	100,000	100,000	200,000
Salaries:			
James	20,500	0	20,500
Kenzie	25,000	25,000	50,000
Lewis	0	0	0
Interest on capital:			
James	1,500	0	1,500
Kenzie	1,500	1,500	3,000
Lewis	1,500	1,500	3,000
Profit available for distribution	50,000	72,000	122,000

Profit share:			
James	30,000	0	30,000
Kenzie	10,000	54,000	64,000
Lewis	10,000	18,000	28,000
Total profit distributed	50,000	72,000	122,000

(b) Current accounts

	James £	Kenzie £	Lewis £		James £	Kenzie £	Lewis £
Balance b/d	800	0	0	Balance b/d	0	3,000	8,600
Drawings	32,000	80,000	26,000	Salaries	16,500	36,000	0
Balance c/d	10,700	5,000	4,600	Interest on capital	3,000	6,000	6,000
				Profit share	24,000	40,000	16,000
	43,500	85,000	30,600		43,500	85,000	30,600

Task 6

(a)

Aldo	£	7,866 (366 + 7,500)	Working: £366 + £7,500
Billy	£	8,100 (600 + 7,500)	Working: £600 + £7,500

(b) **Jasper Partnership**
Statement of financial position as at 31 March 20X1

	Cost £	Depreciation £	Carrying amount £
Non-current assets			
Motor vehicles at cost	43,500	12,125	31,375
Current assets			
Inventory		20,570	
Trade receivables (53,765 – 830)		52,935	
Bank		4,276	
Cash		690	
		78,471	
Current liabilities			
Trade payables	32,950		
VAT	4,740		
Accruals	1,190		
		38,880	
Net current assets			39,591
Net assets			70,966

Financed by:	Aldo	Billy	Total
Capital accounts	35,000	20,000	55,000
Current accounts	7,866	8,100	15,966
	42,866	28,100	70,966

(c) ☐ 1

☐ 2

☐ 3

☑ 4

Notes